Werner Philipp

# We Saw His Star in the East

## How the Operation of an Astronomical Observatory Promotes a Fruitful Discourse Between Faith and Science

Fromm Verlag

**Impressum / Imprint**
Bibliografische Information der Deutschen Nationalbibliothek: Die Deutsche Nationalbibliothek verzeichnet diese Publikation in der Deutschen Nationalbibliografie; detaillierte bibliografische Daten sind im Internet über http://dnb.d-nb.de abrufbar.


Bibliographic information published by the Deutsche Nationalbibliothek: The Deutsche Nationalbibliothek lists this publication in the Deutsche Nationalbibliografie; detailed bibliographic data are available in the Internet at http://dnb.d-nb.de.


Coverbild / Cover image: www.ingimage.com

Verlag / Publisher:
Fromm Verlag
ist ein Imprint der / is a trademark of
AV Akademikerverlag GmbH & Co. KG
Heinrich-Böcking-Str. 6-8, 66121 Saarbrücken, Deutschland / Germany
Email: info@frommverlag.de

Herstellung: siehe letzte Seite /
Printed at: see last page
**ISBN: 978-3-8416-0360-9**

Zugl. / Approved by: Washington DC, Wesley Theological Seminary, Diss., 2012

# ABSTRACT

This dissertation explains how the reconstruction and operation of an astronomical observatory can be a model for the church's missionary work *with* the mostly secularized intellectuals in Dresden. The author analyzes the manifold astronomical references in the Bible and discusses systematic-theological approaches in order to create a fruitful dialogue between Christian Faith and natural science.

## TABLE OF CONTENTS

# INTRODUCTION

**When I look at the night sky and see the work of your fingers – the moon and the stars you set in place – what are mere mortals that you should think about them, human beings that you should care for them? (Psalm 8:3-4, NLT)**

Since my youth I have experienced the same amazement like the Psalmist had when he looked at the starry night sky. The astronomy education at school was the starting point for my big interest in the celestial bodies which became a passionate hobby for many years. I remember, in the beginning of my observations I felt like "a gypsy at the edge of the universe" (Jacques Monod). Then I became a Christian and the impressions during the view of the starry firmament changed into that amazement which perceives the immensity of the universe as an expression of the greatness of God who nevertheless loves every little creature on Earth.

I grew up during the communist regime in East Germany. The education at school was, like all aspects of social life, permeated by the ideological indoctrination of Marxism-Leninism which claimed an avid materialism against any faith in a Creator God above the starry sky. Faith and natural science seemed to be completely separate areas. To work as a teacher or natural scientist was mostly not possible for confessing Christians. Otherwise many teachers and scientists were often alienated from Christian faith and the church.

The fall of Iron Curtain in 1989 completely changed the social system in East Germany into a democratic system according to the Western pattern. The freedom of opinion and belief is guaranteed in all areas. But till now the churches were not able to stop the growing alienation from Christian faith and to decrease the enormous number of people who withdrew their membership. Today East Germany is one of those regions in Europe with the highest secularization, especially among intellectuals. Therefore the church is challenged to stop their self-marginalisation and look for new possibilities of public discourse with this audience in order to implement with them its mission. Dresden with its great economical, educational and cultural possibilities and the relatively large number of intellectuals in the Emmaus UMC who also look for orientation in a secular society provide a unique chance for dialogue between Christian faith and natural science related to astronomy.

In April 2009 there emerged the opportunity to renovate and operate an old astronomical observatory on the edge of Dresden. This dissertation narrates and reflects upon the wonderful story of how this project brought Christians and non-Christians together for a common goal and how the view of the starry firmament and the look into the Bible has raised questions, aroused amazement and provided answers to at least some questions. Like the magi in the Christmas story we are still on the road together - asking, doubting and hoping that we will see the Star in the East and that many will come along to worship Him.

The first chapter of this dissertation will describe the congregational profile of the Emmaus United Methodist Church (UMC) considering its history, ministry and spirituality as a starting point for the necessity and rich possibilities for promoting community outreach and dialogue between Christian faith and secular culture.

The latter will be described in the second chapter where I analyze the special social and religious situation in Dresden and in East Germany in general. This part of my thesis will show the consequences for the public role of the church and its mission in a predominantly atheistic society.

Chapters three to five present the theological foundation of the dialogue between Christian faith and natural science, exemplified by the subject of astronomy. The exegesis of astronomical references in the Bible, their systematic-theological analyses and the approach of a contextual theology essentially shape the form and content of the dialogue between Christian and non-Christian intellectuals.

The sixth chapter narrates the origin and the progress of the observatory project and describes the local and organizational setting of the discourse. Finally, the seventh chapter is about the methods and subjects of the dialogue and reflects on its goal.

## CHAPTER ONE
## THE CONGREGATIONAL PROFILE
## OF DRESDEN EMMAUS UMC

### The History of the Congregation[1]

The Emmaus United Methodist Church in Dresden was founded in 1886 by active lay people, originally as the first Evangelical United Brethren Church. At that time Dresden was the prospering capital of the Kingdom of Saxony (which was a part of the German Empire from 1871) with almost 400,000 inhabitants and a major center of economy, culture and military. The rulers of Dresden were very interested in arts and sciences and supported a fruitful discourse between these different areas. Thus to establish a dialogue between faith and the natural sciences in this place can draw on historical roots and examples.

Regarding certain churchly groups the city government was not so open-minded and tolerant: When the congregation started the members had to meet each other at different apartments or rented saloons. There they held services, Sunday school, Bible study and prayer meetings. The government and the established churches often discriminated against the congregation. But the people were very courageous and missionary and the congregation grew fast. Soon three more congregations were founded in the city and generated a circuit with this church as the main congregation. The first pastor of the congregation, Rev. Bernhard Beck, began his ministry in 1902, 16 years after the church have been founded. This shows that outreach and church planting in the earliest years were essentially initiated by lay people.

In 1907, over 20 years after the foundation of the congregation, a new church building was finished due to a great willingness of the members to make sacrifices. At that time the government approved only a church building

[1] The following data are available on the website of the Emmaus UMC:
http://www.gbz-emmaus.de/geschichte.php
last access: 4 December 2011

hidden away in the court yard and without a bell tower which demonstrated that churches not belonging to one of the state churches were discriminated against. Rev. Wilhelm Quack and the congregation council chose the name "Emmaus Church" for the neo-Gothic styled church. With reference to the Emmaus story in the New Testament the church should be a place where people are able to encounter the resurrected Lord. The theological chapter of this thesis will show that the reference to the resurrection of Jesus Christ can enrich the dialogue between theology and natural science by raising eschatological questions regarding creation and new creation.

In the last century the city experienced the consequences of two world wars started by the Germans. These wars revealed the terrible misuse of science and technology in order to oppress and to kill people in undreamed-of dimensions. Especially this danger of war shows the necessity of an ethical framework for science, research and technology. During World War I the church chronicle complained that most of the men of the congregation had to serve in the military on the front so that only "old men, women and children" attended service. The often fatherless families in the congregation experienced hunger and hardship. At that time the church tried to help by supporting measures and "stationing deaconesses" who visited the families at home and served sacrificially in order to relieve the distress. In 1933 the National Socialists came to power. During the time of National Socialism in the congregation there were many conflicts and arguments about the adoration of Adolf Hitler, anti-Semitism and extermination of the Jews. Especially the latter inhuman crime was realized in the concentration camps right up to technical perfection. Six million Jews were killed, including in prisons and camps near Dresden. Not surprisingly, the chronicle is silent about the attitude of the majority of church members.

In the last days of World War II Dresden was almost completely destroyed. After the war many people of the city suffered from hunger, poverty and sickness. At that time the Emmaus Church was known as a centre of

Christian social welfare work. By the support of the worldwide Methodist church the congregation could offer first aid and helped by alleviating distress and misery. In this way many people in Dresden got to know Methodism and came to the church regularly, including many children. Till today the Emmaus Church wants to be a place of Christian solidarity and charity for all generations. Currently we look for new ways of social outreach. In order to support children in and outside the church we are in the process of planning a ministry of tutoring after the school lessons. Education is an important issue regarding the future professional chances of children and youths. Already at an early age they also can learn that faith and science belong together.

In the last decades the congregation faced various times of crisis and changes. For instance at the end of the sixties and in the seventies the congregation declined more and more. In the beginning of the eighties only 30 people on average attended the service. There were very few children and youth at that time. The two sister congregations which belonged to the circuit were closed. Besides, during the Communist Regime in East Germany Christians were discriminated against in many ways. So they couldn't choose freely a course of study or profession and seldom got a job as white collar employees, teachers or scientists. Additionally, it was not possible to put money aside for renovating the church building. There was a comprehensive deterioration. Then, in 1986 during the tenure of Rev. Eduard Riedner a charismatic awakening started characterized by the practice of charismas, contemporary praise music and intensive evangelization. Many young people and families came to the congregation. The church grew rapidly up again to almost 400 people.

In 1989 the miracle of the political change happened. Dresden and especially the churches there were centres of the peaceful revolution. In 1990 Germany was reunified; Dresden has become one of the most prospering cities in East Germany. The changing of the political system made it possible that the Emmaus Church could be comprehensively renovated from 1991-1994.

Trusting in God the congregation dared to renovate the church for 1.3 million German Marks (about 665,000 Euros). Miraculously, the city government paid 85 percent of the costs. A dark and ramshackle church building became a bright, modern, technically well equipped church with much space and opportunities for meetings, services, ministries and conferences. Today the Emmaus Church is a well known spiritual centre of the city with an active congregation and much space for ecumenical events. Meanwhile the loans of renovation of the Emmaus Church in the nineties are completely paid off.

Finally, it should not go unmentioned that the Emmaus Church also made Methodist history in East Germany. In 1968 when the world wide United Methodist Church was created by the unification of the Evangelical United Brethren Church and The Methodist Church the association service of the East German Annual Conference took place in the Emmaus Church in Dresden. Forty years later I was a delegate to the General Conference in Fort Worth/Texas and could celebrate at the original place of foundation of the worldwide UMC the 40th anniversary of the unification. The theme of the General Conference was “A future with hope – Making disciples for Jesus Christ for the transformation of the world”. The Emmaus UMC is proud to be a part of our worldwide Methodist Church, looks for new horizons and accepts the challenge in a modern city and atheistic society. But to fulfil this task we require a new missional understanding of the church and its ministries in different areas, e.g. the engagement in the dialogue with natural science.

## The Membership and Its Spirituality

The awakening in 1986 attracted mostly members of other churches, particularly former Lutherans. The result of this charismatic change was an enormous growth of the membership of the Emmaus UMC up to almost 400 people. In the last decade the membership of the congregation was stable but also stagnated. Statistically, there was neither a significant increase nor a decrease of people.

Currently there are 206 professing members ("Kirchenglieder"), 45 baptized members ("Angehörige"), 92 unbaptized members ("Zugehörige" [children with baptism deferral]) and 20 friends so that the congregation includes altogether 363 people. The age pyramid of the congregation confirms a balanced presence of all generations, especially a pleasing participation of the young generation. The Emmaus UMC involves 83 children up to 13 (24 percent), 27 youths between 14 and 18 years (8 percent), 58 young adults of 19-30 years (17 percent), 143 adults of 31-60 years (40 percent) and 39 seniors older than 60 years (11 percent). The majority of the membership consists of young families (mostly with 2-4 children) but there are also some young singles up to 45 years (about 10 percent) and 5 elderly widows/ widower up to 97 years.[2] Two-thirds of the members live in Dresden; the remainder comes from 16 surrounding towns and villages up to 30 miles away.

In view of nationality and status the membership is mostly German and has a middle class background. Almost 20 percent of the members work in the areas of management or have other white-collar jobs. Among them there are about 20 people who work in the area of education, science and research. Almost 10 percent of those who belong to the congregation are students. Three percent of the membership came from other countries (Brazil, Bulgaria, Cameroon, Egypt, Great Britain, Poland, USA). Almost all of these people are well educated too and work as teachers, scientists and researchers. It is noticeable that especially the people of the middle class were mostly affected by the social changes of the last years. Many of them are afraid of losing their jobs due to the international financial crisis. But currently only about 2 percent of the people in the congregation are really needy and depend on social welfare.

The **spirituality** of the Emmaus UMC in Dresden is predominantly influenced by the charismatic movement of the 1980s and mostly focused on internal

[2] effective December 2011

practises of charismas. The congregational life appears on the surface to be very active: Today approximately 230 people of all ages regularly attend the one Sunday service including traditional and contemporary music. There are 10 Bible-study groups in the members' homes throughout the city, 4 praise bands, 1 traditional choir, 1 brass choir, 5 children's groups, 3 prayer teams, 1 youth group, 1 men's group, 2 women's groups and other ministries, e.g. for outreach. Except for the ministry of the pastor the whole work in the congregation is on a voluntary basis, e.g. by 7 lay preachers. There are many volunteers, men and women, who serve equally in various ministries.

Despite these impressive numbers there is a gap between the congregation's core values of being a spiritually-centred, missionary-oriented and hospitably-communicative church[3] and its real impact on its environment and the public life. Both the widespread atheism in the East German society and the outstanding academic and cultural potential of the city would require a more open understanding of the Holy Spirit and its gifts which also recognizes its revelation in the sciences and arts and promote a fruitful discourse with the reality outside the church. Although a significant amount of people are working as teachers, professors, and scientists many of these people do not apply the same type of critical thinking to their faith that they do in their work. Work and faith seem to be two disconnected worlds. Religion seems to be relevant only for a small part of their personal lives, especially for individual problems and crises. Therefore the intellectual potential is mostly unused for community outreach. At the same time the relatively high percentage of intellectuals within the membership and the many academic and cultural offerings in the city are a great chance to initiate a dialogue between Christian faith and the surrounding secular culture.

[3] Cf. Mission Statement of the Emmaus UMC, 2008

## Striving for a New Vision

The Emmaus UMC in Dresden experienced a revival 25 years ago and grew more and more in the following years. But now the congregation has arrived at the point of maintenance and is in some areas even declining. According to the life cycle of an organization the phase of maintenance[4] is characterized by a stable and successful congregational work but also by focusing on the complex structures and sustenance of their own flock rather than following the original or a new vision. Indeed, in the last eight to ten years there were only a few new members. There are many groups and ministries but they often do not interact with one another. In the last five years since I have been the pastor in the Emmaus Church my ministry has included mostly administration and the planning and implementation of different events without a clear vision. It became more and more obvious that a renewed vision is very necessary in order for the congregation to stay alive and get a new orientation. It would help to connect more people, ministries and groups in the congregation and make the work more efficient. Furthermore a renewed vision is important in order to maintain a lively contact with the social and cultural environment and to fulfil the congregation's mission in the city.

In 2008 the congregation council developed the following **mission statement**: "First, we want to be a spiritually alive congregation where all people can encounter the word and love of Jesus Christ. Second, we also want to be a missionary church and proclaim the gospel to all people in our city. Third, we claim to be an open church and a hospitable congregation where all people are welcome."[5] This was a good starting point to continue the visioning process in order to discover a new concrete vision which describes what God is calling us to do in the near future to promote our mission. My special task as a leader was to define the reality, to look for clues and to support the discerning and articulation of the vision. I had to realize

---

[4] Cf. Lovett H. Weems, *Take the next step: Leading lasting change in the Church*, (Nashville, TN: Abingdon Press, 2003), 76f.

[5] Mission Statement of the Emmaus UMC in Dresden, 2008

more clearly the needs of the congregation and its environment, to discover the positive and negative indicators for visioning and to help people to describe and implement the dream of God's preferred future. I learnt that this process needs a primarily positive conversation with the people of the congregation, a constructive criticism and supporting people who may have difficulties with possible changes. I discovered more and more that one important area of church leadership is helping the congregation to find this new vision and motivate people to take the next step. Most important for me was the theological reason of a vision that God is not limited to the past or the present but always has a 'not yet' for every congregation. I also encountered this importance of the future for the present in the dialogue between natural science and eschatology.

All these insights led me in 2009 to the decision to establish a **task force** which dealt with the question of a new vision. This team of six people who are either members of the congregation council, stakeholders or experts, discussed and evaluated the ministry of the congregation and related it to the mission statement. The first impression of the team was that whereas we have a strong emphasis on worship, children/youth ministry and prayer groups we lack Christian education for adults, goal oriented outreach and social work. The team also listed every group, activity and event, analyzed the membership and its capabilities and evaluated the Sunday service attendance. The result was that there are over 40 groups and ministries, 65 percent of the members attend the Sunday service, 30 percent of the membership is involved in a ministry or small group but only 5 percent of the members are engaged in outreach programs. We noticed that five new projects have started in the last four years: "Totale Offensive-B.L.O.C.K.G" – a soccer fan ministry (2007), a "Cyclist Mission" on the cycleway along the river Elbe (2007), the guest service "John's construction" (2009), a special prayer and blessing service for sick people (2009), and the astronomical observatory project (2009). But the first three mission projects have been suspended or have ended already so that most of the congregation's activities still serve the established membership rather than seekers inside and outside of the church. The astronomical observatory project is currently the only public project supported by our congregation. Is builds a bridge to people outside the church and forces the dialogue between church and a special area of the surrounding culture. Since the beginning of this project the task force has always mentored, advised and evaluated the activities and development of the observatory project. Thereby it has become obvious that its perpetuation could be an important part of a new vision which changes the uneven relation between “indoor service” and outreach.

# CHAPTER TWO
# THE SOCIAL AND RELIGIOUS ENVIRONMENT

## The Urban Setting of Dresden

Dresden[6] is the capital of the German Federal State of Saxony and has currently 524,233 inhabitants. It is one of the most prosperous cities in East Germany in demographical, economical, academic and cultural respects. **Demographically**, Dresden is one of the very few East German cities whose population has been increasing in the last years (12 percent since 1999). The reasons are the highest birth rate in Germany (110 babies per 10,000 inhabitants)[7] and a permanent influx. This is in contrast to the general trend in East Germany where the population has been steadily decreasing since the reunification in 1990. The city has 20,982 foreigners (= 4.1 per cent of the population). The population density is 1,575 people per square kilometre.

**Economically**, Dresden has developed into one of Germany's strongest and most dynamic locations. The city is debt-free and with an economical growth of 22.2 percent since 2000, lies well above the national average. Dresden today is one of the most dynamic high-tech locations in Europe, with a particular emphasis on microelectronics, IT and telecommunications, biotechnology, nanotechnology, photovoltaics and the development and manufacturing of new materials. Further traditional cornerstones are mechanical engineering and plant construction, aircraft and automobile manufacturing, printing, pharmaceuticals and the food and drink industry. 1,200 companies with more than 40,000 employees make Dresden the largest European microelectronics and ICT cluster, called "Silicon Saxony".[8]

---

[6] The following data you find in: Landeshauptstadt Dresden, *Focus on Dresden: The capital of Saxony in figures – 2011* (Dresden: designXpress dresden , 19th [updated] ed., April 2011), 9ff.
[7] http://www.dresden.de/media/pdf/statistik/Dresdner_Zahlen_aktuell_17_2010_07.pdf last access: 10 December 2011
[8] Landeshauptstadt Dresden, ibid., 12.

Dresden is an important centre of **education and science**. The city is considered as one of the most long-standing location of applied research and engineering in the German speaking countries.[9] The pioneering role in these areas has historical roots in the early modern age. Already in 1712 the first autonomous Saxon engineer corps was founded within the military composed of people with special scientific knowledge and technological competence in architecture, mining, melioration, road and bridge building, geodesy and cartography.[10] From this have emerged various engineering academies, colleges of technology, and in 1828 the Dresden University of Technology which has today 35,000 students. Famous professors and engineers taught and worked in Dresden: Johann Andreas Schubert (1808-1870) developed the first German locomotive, the first paddle steamer on the river Elbe (1837) and the worldwide largest brick bridge (Göltzschtalbrücke). Gustav-Anton Zeuner (1828-1907) was a famous professor of technical mechanics and actively supported the implementation of the human sciences too. Heinrich Barkhausen (1881-1956) and Nikolaus Joachim Lehmann (1921-1998) were pioneers in the history of electronics.[11] And Manfred von Ardenne (1907-1997) invented the tube television and the electron microscope among many others patents.[12]

Today, the city has 133 municipal schools, 43 independent schools and 3 state-run schools with 63,115 pupils.[13] It is considered as the strongest research location in Eastern Germany. Important institutions in the area of technology and science are next to the Dresden University of Technology, the

---

[9] Thomas Hänseroth, *"Nützliche Wissenschaften" in Dresden im 18. und frühen 19.Jahrhundert*, in: *Dresden – Stadt der Wissenschaften, Dresdner Hefte Nr.86*, (Dresden: Grafischer Betrieb und Verlagsgesellschaft mbH, 2006), 5ff.

[10] Thomas Hänseroth, ibid., 10ff.

[11] Klaus Mauersberger, *Große Köpfe Dresdner Ingenieurwissenschaften*, in: *Dresden – Stadt der Wissenschaften, Dresdner Hefte Nr.86*, (Dresden: Grafischer Betrieb und Verlagsgesellschaft mbH, 2006), 15ff.

[12] Friedrich Diekmann, *Die unbegriffene Elbhangkugel: Manfred von Ardenne in Sinop und in Dresden*, in: *Dresden – Stadt der Wissenschaften, Dresdner Hefte Nr.86*, (Dresden: Grafischer Betrieb und Verlagsgesellschaft mbH, 2006), 27ff.

[13] Landeshauptstadt Dresden, ibid., 18.

HTW Dresden University of Applied Sciences, 11 institutes of the Fraunhofer Society, 3 institutes of the Max Planck Society, 5 institutes of the Leibniz Association, 1 research centre of the German Research Foundation (Helmholtz Association), the BioInnovationCentre Dresden, the Max Bergmann Centre for Biomaterials, the NanoelectronicsCentre Dresden, and the Dresden Technology Centre.[14] These innovative research institutes are widely connected to other international research centres and companies. The growing scientific network and economical globalization influence the development of the city.

**Culturally,** the 800 year-old city unites cultural and art treasures of European renown. In addition to the historical architecture of the city there are 44 museums, 56 galleries and exhibitions, 87 libraries and archives, 36 theatres and stages and world famous musical ensembles and institutions. Throughout the history economy and culture created a unique symbiosis in Dresden. Every year the city attracts about 10 million visitors and tourists.

But Dresden also has the typical problems of an East German city. After the fall of the Iron Curtain the people in East Germany experienced a complete change in the former **social system.** They have got the freedoms of a democratic political system but they are also faced with its social problems. For instance the unemployment rate is 11.2 percent and almost 59,000 people are on welfare[15]. Families with many children are often affected by a higher poverty risk. Young people sometimes have trouble getting an apprenticeship or abuse alcohol and drugs. Generally, the divide between rich and poor is growing. In addition, there is also a latent xenophobia.

The Emmaus Church is situated in the district of Dresden called **"Neustadt"**, which is only one mile from downtown. The district "Neustadt"[16] has 16,157

---

[14] Landeshauptstadt Dresden, ibid., 12f.

[15] http://www.dresden.de/media/pdf/statistik/Dresdner_Zahlen_aktuell_17_2010_07.pdf last access: 10 December 2011

[16] The following data see: http://www.dresden.de/media/pdf/statistik/11__ussere_Neustadt.pdf last access: 10 December 2011

inhabitants (including 8.1 percent foreigners). It is a multicultural district with many students and young families (70.1 percent are never married singles; the average age of the population is 31.5 years). Near the church there are 4 theaters/cinemas, 7 hotels and almost 200 taverns (within one square kilometre!) It is known as the entertainment district of Dresden. In the district there is a higher than usual percentage of children and youths (14.4 percent under 18 years) so that you can find 7 kindergartens, 4 schools and 13 other facilities for this age group. During the German Democratic Republic (GDR) regime and immediately following the reunification the district was a social hot spot. Although currently there is 9.0 percent unemployment and 15.2 percent of the population is on welfare, the economical, social and cultural levels have increased significantly in the last years. Today Dresden-Neustadt is a modern district with a high standard of living.

**In summary:** The urban profile shows some possibilities and needs which the astronomical observatory project should be aware of. **First,** Dresden is a prospering centre of science and research in East Germany. Therefore this city is an ideal location for dealing with the questions of how faith and science are connected and how we can arouse interest in Christian faith among intellectuals. Some people in the congregation work at schools, universities and research facilities too and can contribute their knowledge and experiences in this issue. The astronomical observatory project is a great chance to bring Christian and non-Christian intellectuals together in order to initiate a fruitful dialogue between faith and science.

**Second,** Dresden is characterized by an expanding economy as well as significant social problems. The growing difference between rich and poor in our society doesn't go without notice. The dialogue between faith and science also needs to address questions of power, globalization and social justice. A project like the astronomical observatory can bring together people of different social classes in order to discuss the social implications of faith and science. Another relevant subject connected to the growing economy of a prospering city is sustainability and environmental protection. Faith and science are also linked to this ethical question of how we deal with natural resources and contribute to the integrity of creation.

**Third**, Dresden's population is significantly growing due to outsiders relocating and a higher birth rate. This is an important indication that there is an outstanding amount of young people in the city. The astronomical observatory project should offer activities which especially invite children, youths and young families and should pay attention to their social needs, e.g. in view of education.

**Fourth**, Dresden is abounding in culture and arts. The relationship between natural science, arts and religion was characteristic for Dresden in the last centuries and shaped its culture. All three areas often fertilized each other throughout history and made the city into a very innovative location. But since the heliocentric turnaround in the modern age the poet and the scientist have become more and more separated.[17] However, today we recognize again that the scientific worldview needs to be supplemented by an aesthetic component.[18] Thus arts could be a meeting point or a bridge between natural science and religion. All three areas should be considered as independent but not separate expressions of the one reality.

## The Religious Situation in East Germany

The religious situation in East Germany is marked by a wide spread atheism. About 70 percent of the population is completely non-religious. "This country became a really post-Christian culture".[19] Most of the people have no idea of

[17] Ernst-Peter Fischer, *Von ästhetischen Momenten und poetischen Potentialen der Wissenschaft*, in: *Dresden – Stadt der Wissenschaften, Dresdner Hefte Nr.86*, (Dresden: Grafischer Betrieb und Verlagsgesellschaft mbH, 2006), 90.

[18] Ernst-Peter Fischer, ibid., 92.

[19] Tomka, Miklós, Zulehner Paul, *Religion in den Reformländern Ost- (Mittel)Europas*,

any god. “If Western Europe is like a churchly disaster area, then East Germany is the epicentre, or using another picture – it is situated in the umbral shadow of the ‘darkness of God’ which was prophesied by Marx and Nietzsche and emphatically described by Buber.”[20] The religious situation in East Germany has also been called “transcendental homelessness”.[21] A widespread spiritual emptiness and indifference are very characteristic. Regarding our subject it is important to notice that many people in the highly secularized society of East Germany take for granted an antagonism between science and religion. In the former GDR this conviction was even a public doctrine implemented and taught in all schools and universities. The Communist ideology of the GDR asserted a clear contradiction between religion and natural science. To be a competent scientist often meant to be a convinced atheist. Religion was considered as a relic of an antiquated and backward worldview. Many intellectuals who grew up and worked in the former GDR still have this conviction. Nowadays adherents of the so called “New Atheism” assert again a contradiction between natural science and religion that maintains this thinking.[22]

But there is also a crisis within the churches and an inability to meet the needs of the secularized people and to be present in the public. Since 1989 over 7 million Germans have left the churches[23] or are shattered in their confession. Most of them live in East Germany. Many Christians are alienated from their spiritual and traditional roots. For example a survey shows that only 61 percent of Catholics and 48 percent of Protestants believe in the

(Wien/Ostfildern: Schwabenverlag, 1999), 177; translation German-English made by myself.

[20] Eberhard Tiefensee in: Tabea Sporer, *Konfessionslosigkeit ein Ostdeutsches Phänomen?* in: Christen in der Offensive e.V. Reichelsheim (Hrsg.), *Brennpunkt Seelsorge, Heft 1/2003*, 4.

[21] The term was created by Georg Lukács, *Theorie des Romans*, 1994, 32 cited in: Lutz Friedrich, *Autobiographie und Religion der Spätmoderne: Biographische Suchbewegungen im Zeitalter transzendentaler Obdachlosigkeit*, (Stuttgart: Kohlhammer, 1999), 8.

[22] Patrick Becker, *Kein Platz für Gott? Theologie im Zeitalter der Naturwissenschaften*, (Regensburg: Verlag Heinrich Pustet, 2009), 10.

[23] http://www.kirchenaustritt.de/statistik/#Religionszugehoerigkeit_in_Deutschland last access: 10 December 2011

resurrection of Jesus Christ.[24] It is typical that also in Dresden only 25 percent of the population are Christians and less than 1 percent members of other religions.[25] Christians by denominations located in Dresden are e.g. Lutheran: 78,966 (15.3 percent), Catholic 22,190 (4.3 percent), and free churches 25,130 (4.8 percent). Among the latter there are 4 United Methodist Churches with a membership of 757 people.[26] In addition there is a Jewish community (building and consecration of the new synagogue in 2001, 350 members = 0.07 percent) and three Islamic communities (600 Moslems = 0.1 percent). The inner crisis of the churches often leads to their self-marginalization and less public relevance in society.

## Consequences for the Public Role of the Church

A project which deals with dialogue between Christian faith and natural science has to take seriously this very special religious situation in East Germany, and the public role of the church in this context. **First, the church has to assert itself within a post-Christian society and culture. Church leadership in that context means to be aware of a minority position which is called to public dialogue.** As Christians we are called to follow the Lord and proclaim the gospel within a secular world, not outside of it. "The church must come out of its stagnation. We must move out again into the open air of intellectual discussion with the world, and risk saying controversial things, if we are to get down to the serious business of life."[27] The astronomical observatory project is a great possibility to make contact with people of different intellectual, social, cultural and ideological backgrounds

---

[24] Hanspeter Oschwald, *Glaube in Deutschland*, (München: Focus/Meyers Lexikonverlag, 1999), 20f.
[25] Landeshauptstadt Dresden, ibid., 9.
http://www.dresden.de/de/03/kirchen.php
last access: 10 December 2011
[26] Evangelisch-methodistische Kirche, *OJK, Verhandlungen der 44.Tagung gehalten in Crottendorf 25.Mai-29.Mai 2011: Statistik des Jahres 2010*, 2.
[27] Dietrich Bonhoeffer, *Letters and Papers from Prison*, ed. Eberhard Bethge (New York: Touchstone, 1997), 378.

and discuss scientific and theological questions in an open intellectual atmosphere. Thereby the conversation with non-Christians needs to be characterized by respect, honesty, and readiness of learning from each other. The conversation with non-Christians in the East German context requires the acceptance of our own minority position and the readiness to be a public leader without publicity. It is important to recognize that this dialogue has its own worth and should not be misinterpreted as an attempt to quickly get people into the church like the next insight will show.

**Second, our big challenge today is not the question of church but the question of God.**[28] **To be a church leader in the public means to be a theologian who addresses and interprets experiences of God in our predominately atheistic society.** The prior theological question in our post-Christian context is not how the church will be able to survive or get more members. It is not primarily about more effective structure of the church or for better methods of evangelization. Rather we are confronted with the radical question of God and the need to discover where the question for God is explicitly or implicitly present among the people. The atheistic experience of spiritual emptiness could be a link for the hidden search for God or for the meaning of life. We should ask together (!) with the non-Christian for the "ultimate concern" (Paul Tillich). It is particularly important to recognize that Christian faith is not only relevant for individual salvation but for our worldly life in human society. The question of God also needs to be addressed beyond experiences of human limits and crises:

> Religious people speak of God when human knowledge (perhaps simply because they are too lazy to think) has come to an end, or when human resources fail – in fact it is always the deus ex

---

[28] Joachim Wanke in: Hrsg. EMW, ACK, Missio, *Aufbruch zu einer missionarischen Ökumene: Ein Verständigungsprozess über die gemeinsame Aufgabe der Mission und Evangelisation in Deutschland*, (Hamburg: Breklumer Druckerei Manfred Siegel KG, 1999), 138; translation German - English made by myself.

> machina that they bring on to the scene, either for the apparent solution of insoluble problems, or as strength in failure – always, that is to say, exploiting human weakness or human boundaries.... As to the boundaries, it seems to me better to be silent and leave the insoluble unsolved.... God is beyond the midst of our life. The Church stands, not at the boundaries where human powers give out, but in the middle of the village.[29]

In fact, we need to proclaim the Gospel and the relevance of Christian faith in the midst of people's life and society and not only when the limits of knowledge and existence appear.
The astronomical observatory project is a great chance to support the communication of the gospel in our post-Christian culture by initiating an intensive dialogue between Christians and non-Christians in daily life and a collaboration for a project of common interest. The subject 'astronomy' is very abundant in theological and philosophical references so that it is easy to address the question of God. From that point topics like the belief in a Creator God, the meaning of our life in the universe and our responsibility for the blue planet Earth are obvious. The people, both atheists and Christians, face the question of God directly and indirectly in the midst of their daily lives and interests and not only on their boundaries, and recognize its personal and social relevance. The dialogue between religion and natural science is a special platform to show that Christians don't believe in a God of the gaps but in the omnipresent creator.
**Third, the church needs to proclaim the gospel understandably in the context of a non-religious society. Public church leadership is called to speak about God in non-religious ways.**

---

[29] Dietrich Bonhoeffer, 281f.

There is a great challenge for Christians and church leaders to speak understandably about God with people in a mostly atheistic society. Common starting points like basic knowledge of Christian faith, similar religious traditions, and shared values are scarcely available. There is a need to translate the gospel into a secular language and teach Christians to speak about God a-religiously. The priesthood of all believers requires mature believers who can express understandably and contemporarily their creed and faith experiences. We need to develop new "secular shapes of evangelization".[30]

The atheistic society in East Germany requires something like "religionless Christianity" (Dietrich Bonhoeffer) which does not mean faith or theology without God but a rejection of the metaphysical God (as 'deus ex machina' or as working hypothesis) of false religion: "We have to live in the world *etsi deus non daretur* and this is just what we do recognize - before God! ...The God who lets us live in the world without the working hypothesis of God is the God before whom we stand continually. Before God and with God we live without God."[31] This concept could be very relevant not only for Christians in an atheistic society in general but especially for Christian teachers, engineers or scientists who have to deal with a (necessary) methodical atheism as well as an atheistic social environment which seemingly often contradicts religious belief. But a worldly life or profession doesn't exclude being a convinced Christian. The consequence is not a life without deep spirituality but rather a "secret discipline" (Arkandisziplin)[32], or as Karl Rahner wrote: "The Christian of the future will be a mystic or he [or she] will not exist."[33] This "secret discipline" or mystic of everyday life will meet Christ in the world; this includes the world of atheists and their questions and needs. Both the worldly life and

[30] Miloslav Kardinal Vlk, Also *avanti! -Christentum und Kirche im Gegenwind der Zeit*, (Leipzig: Benno-Verlag, 1999), 121.
[31] Dietrich Bonhoeffer, ibid., 360.
[32] ibid., 281.
[33] Karl Rahner, *Schriften zur Theologie Bd. VII*, (Einsiedeln: Benzinger, 1966), 22f.

the secret spiritual discipline are dialectical poles of Christian existence and identity which are mutual dependent.

The astronomical observatory project invites Christians who work in the public area as teachers, engineers and scientists to think about and to discuss the concepts of "religionless Christianity" and "non-religious interpretation" of the gospel. They learn to formulate a testimony beyond metaphysical, dominant and individualistic terms and use more concepts like dialogue, freedom, tolerance, participation and solidarity. It is necessary to increase the awareness of our experiences of God in a secular environment and to find an understandable hermeneutic and language to express them in a secular setting. The project challenges reflections on apologetics, which enables one to put oneself in the shoes of non-believers, to ask relevant questions and to give answers of faith to non-Christians but also learn from them! The observatory project is a field of learning, training and experience exchange where we practice the gospel through dialogue, partnership, tolerance and participation.

**Fourth, the church needs a missional understanding of its ministry which recognizes that the congregation is not the goal but the instrument of mission. A church leader looks for new ways of mission "with others".**

The church has a missional identity and calling. "The Church is the Church only when it exists for others...."[34] Therefore we need to leave the comfort zone of our church meetings and events and become more like disciples on a pilgrimage with open ears, eyes and hearts for our sceptical neighbours. Actually, "mission is the call of the church and its deepest identity... it is the basic charisma of the church and therefore an event from above and not a result of human efforts."[35] Because of the wide gap between atheistic society

---

[34] Dietrich Bonhoeffer, 382f.

[35] Mühlen, Heribert, *Neu mit Gott*, (Freiburg: Herder-Verlag, 2000), 20; translation German - English made by myself.

and Christian tradition in East Germany a re-Christianization of the culture is not practical. A call to all Christians for mission because of the shrinking membership of the churches would not be enough. Furthermore, mission needs to become a lifestyle of the church consisting of Christians helping and serving within secular life. Missional leadership in this respect is not only about the church but the Kingdom of God in the secular world. "The church... is not the purpose or goal of the gospel, but rather its instrument and witness."[36] These criticisms make church leaders aware that mission is not only about church growth or church planting but God's work in the world, in society as well as in nature! Additionally, mission today cannot be a one way action but needs to be in collaboration with the people being addressed. The church in a highly secularized context cannot be only 'church *for* others' but needs to be church *with* others. The astronomical observatory project tries to implement this insight: we not only bring something to the people but we work together and discover God's footprints in our world and the universe. To work together with people outside church in a common issue is a great missionary enterprise of giving and taking on both sides. The observatory project shows that participation of non-Christians in our missionary activities as well as the collaboration of Christians with secular organizations are more effective than the founding of missionary task forces and outreach groups which only want to bring people something of the gospel without asking for their engagement. The barrier to entering the congregation in this way is usually very high for non-Christians. A common project can minimize the obstacles and resistance and also help Christians to learn from their environment.

**Fifth, in the age of increasing individualism and privatization, the public role of the church is to provide new ways of fellowship and communion. Public leadership is called to bring people of different social backgrounds together for a common good.** Our society is characterized

[36] Darell L. Guder, *Missional Church*, (Grand Rapids, MI: William B. Erdmann Publishing Company, 1998), 5.

on the one hand by privatization of religion and marginalization of the church and on the other hand by the people's experiences of egoism, loneliness and loss of solidarity. Even within the churches there is a growing tendency of individualization and privatization of faith, also called "ecclesiological atheism".[37] The churchly life should not support such tendencies by one-sided orientation to individual needs and preferences but promote fellowship between people of different ages, races, social classes and strengthen reconciled diversity. The collective character of Christian faith, the image of the church as a body with many parts, and the communal nature of the Triune God lead to a social spirituality and mission. Believing in Jesus includes living in community. Christians are called to fellowship. Personal discipleship doesn't mean individualism leading to a privatized faith independent of the church or of others. There is no doubt that the new life in Christ has a collective nature and sets us in relationship with other believers- and non-believers! The mission of the church has a collaborative character and invites all people of our neighbourhood who often experience social exclusion, marginalization or isolation in their everyday life.

Therefore a church leader should support mission as a collaborative enterprise, whose goal is to embrace diversity and overcome individualization and marginalization. To be a hospitable church cannot only mean that we provide and extend a welcoming face only in the congregation and create space where strangers can enter and become friends. We need to live hospitality, which is oriented to the public realm, make contact with non-Christians, work together with secular organizations in order to get to know strangers and have a dialogue with them. This conversation needs to start with listening because "listening is a form of spiritual hospitality by which you invite strangers to become friends, to get to know their inner selves more

[37] Term created by Bishop Kurt Koch, Switzerland, quoted in: Miloslav Kardinal Vlk, ibid., 123.

fully."[38] In any case, strangers should feel not only as receivers of our message and gifts but also as people who teach us their experiences, share with us their capabilities and actually take part in our mission.

The observatory project is such a collective social activity and not merely an exercise of a common hobby for some interested people. Men and women of different ages, nationalities, professions, social classes and worldviews work together for common good. Christians of Emmaus UMC are active members of the observatory interest group and share their knowledge, capabilities and experiences with other group members. The social component of this project is the offering of extracurricular education and meaningful leisure activities for pupils, especially for children of socially disadvantaged families. So the observatory project is a good example of a common collective effort of Christians and non-Christians to make a small contribution to society. "It is not the religious act that creates the Christian but participation in the sufferings of God in the secular life."[39]

---

[38] Henri.J.M. Nouwen, *Leben hier und jetzt*, (Freiburg: Herder-Verlag, 2000), 84; English Version on the internet: http://www.henrinouwen.org/home/free_eletters
last access: 11 March 2011

[39] Dietrich Bonhoeffer, ibid., 361.

# CHAPTER THREE
# THE BIBLICAL - THEOLOGICAL FOUNDATION

## Astronomical References in the Bible

Looking at the starry sky is a wonderful possibility to look back to the past. According to their distance the light of the stars and the other celestial bodies need different times till meeting our eyes. Some of them are so far that today we receive the light which they have sent at biblical times! On the other hand we know that the same celestial bodies we observe today also shone upon Abraham, David, Job, Isaiah and Jesus. "Astronomy...gives us the power of placing ourselves to some degree in the position of the patriarchs and prophets of old...We can see the unchanging heavens with their eyes, and understand their attitude towards them."[40] But before I present the astronomical references in the Bible I want to describe a little bit the beginnings of astronomy in the nations surrounding Israel in ancient times.

## Astronomy in Babylon and Egypt

Astronomy (Greek: "astron" = star and "nomos" = law) is one of the oldest natural sciences and deals with the observation and the study of the celestial bodies and their movements. In ancient times it was connected to the religious adoration of the Sun, Moon and stars but also used for practical needs like time management (calendar), celestial navigation, meteorology, architecture and agriculture.

Two of the most important birthplaces of astronomy in ancient times were Mesopotamia and Egypt, empires, which were largely linked to the history of Israel. In Babylon[41] astronomical research started around 2000 B.C. and it was always mixed with astrological interpretations. The climax of Babylonian

---

[40] E. Walter Maunder, *The Astronomy of the Bible,* (La Vergne, TN: Wildside Press 1908, ed. 2009), vii.

[41] Cf. A.Weigert, H.Zimmermann, *Brockhaus ABC Astronomie*, (Leipzig: F.A.Brockhaus Verlag, 1976, 7th ed.), 23f.

astronomy was in the fifth and sixth centuries B.C. when the synodic period of visible planets and the eclipse cycles of the Sun and Moon were known so that eclipses became predictable. A highlight of late Babylonian astronomy was the lunar tablets of the astronomer Kiddinu (ca. 380 B.C.) which calculated the first appearance of the crescent Moon after the new Moon. This calculation of the lunar phase cycle (lunation) influenced also the Hebrew Calendar which was a moon based calendar.

In Egypt[42] astronomy probably started around 5000 B.C. (e.g. stone circles at Nabta Playa). The astronomers who were priests like in Babylon dealt mainly with the calculation of the calendar and the fixing of the religious festivals. Already around 3000 B.C. a sun based calendar with 365 days was in use! The heliacal rising of Sirius played a special role in this calendar because it coincided with the deluge of the Nile.[43] The prediction of these natural phenomena was important for the timing of agricultural activities. It seems that also the architecture of the pyramids was connected to astronomical observations. Both Babylonian and Egyptian astronomy were important predecessors of the later astronomy in the Hellenistic and Roman times up to the middle ages.

In the Babylonian and Egyptian empires the celestial bodies were seen as astral deities who influence life on Earth in many ways. In various cults the Sun, Moon and stars were worshipped. Religion and science were still one thing and inseparably mixed. Astronomical insights were merged with astrological interpretations. Powerful rulers and priest classes were in charge to interpret natural and religious reality and used also their knowledge for sustaining their political power and social position. The history of astronomy from its beginnings shows the connection between knowledge and power. The question is always raised who has the prerogative of interpretation of reality. On the one hand science has always been influenced by social,

[42] Cf. ibid., 24f.

[43] Dieter B. Herrmann, *Entdecker des Himmels*, (Leipzig: Urania-Verlag, 1990, 4th ed.), 13.

political and economical forces. On the other hand new scientific insights had consequences for these forces and changed power relations. The dialogue between theology and natural science often has to deal with the question of the prerogative interpretation of reality and power issues because knowledge is power. Therefore the role of astronomy in the "narrative of empire"[44] can be an important part of the dialogue between natural science and theology.

## Astronomy of the Bible

Although astronomical terms and subjects are present in the whole Scripture there is very less new exegetical research and literature about it since decades if not since a century![45] The following presentation of the biblical material can be not a complete description of astronomy in the Bible but only an extract of the relevant passages useable for discourse between theology and natural science. Biblical astronomy includes "the views taken in the books of the Bible of the position of the earth in the universe, the designation of the stars, planets, fixed stars, and the views held regarding them."[46] It examines "the astronomical allusions as occur with respect to their appropriateness to the lesson which the writer desired to teach..., what connection can be traced between the...Scriptures and the Constellations ... [and] the use made of heavenly bodies as time-measurers amongst the Hebrews."[47]

Even if there was a certain amount of interest in the investigation of nature among biblical authors (cf. 1Kgs 4:29-34), especially in the later wisdom literature, the Bible doesn't speak about astronomy in a special way or offer a

---

[44] Daniel E. Groody, *Globalization, Spirituality, and Justice*, (New York, NY: Maryknoll, 2010), 34ff.
[45] A bibliography is available in Georg Fohrer, *Das Buch Hiob. Kommentar zum Alten Testament*, (Berlin: Evangelische Verlagsanstalt GmbH, 1988, 2nd ed.), 198 footnote 9.
The last major study on astronomical references in the Bible is the book of E. Walter Maunder, *The Astronomy of the Bible* from 1908! (La Vergne, TN: Wildside Press 1908, ed. 2009).
[46] http://www.jewishencyclopedia.com/view.jsp?artid=2052&letter=A#6263
last access: 27 September 2011. This website contains the complete contents of the 12-volume Jewish Encyclopedia, which was originally published between 1901-1906.
[47] E.Walter Maunder, ibid., 11.

complete cosmology. Aside from the fact that the astronomical references are not numerous enough and often too ambiguous in order to reconstruct a "biblical astronomy", the Bible would be misunderstood if we would read or use it as an astronomical schoolbook. Texts with astronomical references are based on the knowledge of their time and always connect the observation of nature, in our case of the celestial bodies, with theological statements or spiritual messages. The authors of the biblical books use the mythological worldview of their time and reinterpret them in order to formulate creeds which are connected to God as the creator of heaven and earth. Not by chance we find most of the passages with astronomical terms in the poetic sections of the Bible.

In the following I list the astronomical terms and references in the Bible and try to explain them.

## The Sky, Heaven, Firmament and Universe

The Hebrew word for "heaven" or "sky" is the *plurale tantum* שָׁמַיִם (shamayim) which occurs 420 times in the Old Testament. It probably derives from מַיִם (mayim) which means „water" because the visible sky was seen as the place surrounded by a primordial ocean.[48] According to the ancient three-story worldview שָׁמַיִם (shamayim) is the space above which is separated from the disc of the earth in the midst and the water below and around it. שָׁמַיִם is created by God (Gn 1:1) and describes the space of the celestial bodies as well as the atmosphere (for which there is no Hebrew term) where the meteorological phenomena occur. Theologically it is the divine sphere, where God and his heavenly host dwell. From there he reigns over all powers, gives signs of his revelation and influences the life on earth. But there was also the insight that even the highest heaven cannot contain God

[48] Ernst Jenni/ Claus Westermann, *Theologisches Handwörterbuch zum Alten Testament II*, (München: Chr. Kaiser Verlag, 1984), col. 966.

because he is beyond the cosmic borderlines (1 Kgs 8:27). Although the heaven is a symbol for high stability, the later Scriptures of the Old Testament and the New Testament speak about an end of the heaven (e.g. Is 34:4; 51:6; Job 14:12; Mk 13:31) or its substitution by a new one (2 Pt 3:13; Rv 21:1).

Another similar term for sky or heaven is "firmament", in Hebrew called רָקִיעַ (= raqia: an extended surface, expanse; appears 17 times in the Old Testament).[49] God created this plate and located it between the primordial ocean and the earth (Gn 1:6). Originally it divided the waters above from those beneath. Then the waters on earth were concentrated on special places (Gn 1:9) and the firmament separated the water from above from the earth. It was imagined like a big cover or vault, arching the whole earth and also regulating the precipitation from above. At the same time רָקִיעַ was also the place where the stars and other celestial bodies (Gen.1:14) became fixed (cf. “fixed stars”).

The New Testament uses the term *οὐρανός* (= ouranos: heaven, sky) which obviously includes all meanings of the Old Testament terms too.[50] The word can express likewise natural and spiritual aspects of the subject. *οὐρανός* signifies the visible heavens: the atmosphere, the sky, the starry firmament but also the divine sphere. It seems that the term unites natural, philosophical and religious connotation. In an astronomical respect *οὐρανός* was used for descriptions of outer space and the starry sky (cf. Heb 11:12).

The Old Testament doesn’t have a word for "universe". Usually the phrase "heaven and earth" (or vice versa) means the world as a whole (e.g. Gn.1:1).[51] Remarkable is also the expression "highest heavens" (e.g. Dt 10:14; Ps 148:4). It doesn’t describe the highest sphere of heaven but the sky

---

[49] Ibid., col. 966f.

[50] Walter Bauer, *Wörterbuch zum Neuen Testament*, (Berlin: Walter De Gruyter, 1971), col. 1176ff.

[51] Ernst Jenni/ Claus Westermann, *Theologisches Handwörterbuch zum Alten Testament I*, (München: Chr. Kaiser Verlag, 1984), col. 229f.

or heaven in its totality.[52] In the New Testament we encounter the term *κοσμος* (= cosmos: adornment, also: world, universe, worldly affairs; the inhabitants of the world). In various contexts it can signify the world as a whole, everything that exists or the universe where the stars are (cf. Phil 2:15).[53] Of course, at biblical times there was no scientific knowledge of outer space or the universe as there is today.

**The Sun**

The Sun is mentioned very often in the Bible (Gn 37:9; Jo 10:12; Ps 19:5ff etc.). Many phrases like "under the Sun" (e.g. Eccl 1:3ff) or "as long as the Sun" (e.g. Ps 72:17) or "who see the Sun" (Eccl 7:11) show its general importance for life on earth. It is shining on earth (Gn 14ff), warms it up (1 Sm 11:9; Neh 7:3) but can also be seen negatively as hot and painful (Ps 121:6; Is 49:10; Jon 4:8).[54] Interestingly, the Sun was not seen as the primary light giver. The creation of light (Gn.1:3) before the creation of the celestial bodies could be connected to the demythologizing of Babylonian astral deities.[55] The separation made clear that God is the creator of light as a condition for living in space and time. The light itself but also the light-bearing celestial bodies like the Sun have no divine dignity. Furthermore the light is created by God's word and not an emanation of the deity.[56] The creation of the light but also of the following objects by God's word shows the clear difference between God and creation. On the other hand the divine creating word also demonstrates the relationship between God and his creation.

The Hebrew word for "Sun" is שֶׁמֶשׁ (=shemesh: Sun) occurs 134 times in the Old Testament (not including occurrences in names of persons and

[52] Ibid., *II*: col. 968.
[53] Walter Bauer, ibid., col.881.
[54] Wilhelm Gesenius, *Hebräisches und aramäisches Handwörterbuch über das Alte Testament,* (Berlin: Springer-Verlag, 1962, 17th ed.), 849.
[55] Gerhard von Rad, *Das erste Buch Mose, ATD 2*, (Göttingen: Vandenhoek & Ruprecht, 1949), 39.
[56] Ibid., 39.

localities). Almost all Semitic languages used the same root of the word in order to signify the Sun.[57] But the same word was also a name of a sun deity so that the biblical creation story avoids this term. Furthermore it emphasizes that the Sun is made by God as the "greater light" in order to govern the day and serve for the division of time (Gn 1:14ff; cf. Ps 136:8). For instance, the end and new beginning of a day was defined by the sunset.[58] Additionally, the observation of sunrise and sunset played an important role in the Torah (Ex 22:2ff; Lv 22:7; Dt 16:6; 23:12). The solar orientation of the cardinal directions is a further example of practical astronomy in the Bible: מְבוֹא שֶׁמֶשׁ (= mabo: entrance; e.g. Dt 11,30; Jo 1:4) signify West, מִזְרַח שֶׁמֶשׁ (=mizrach: rises; e.g. Jgs 11:18; Ps 50:1) East. Traditio-historically, the sunrise was connected to righteousness or a just ruler (2 Sm 23:4; Mal 4:2; cf. Mt 5:45).

Theologically significant is the differentiated view of the Sun in the Bible. Especially in poetic texts the Sun is often mentioned regarding the praise of God as the creator (Ps 19:5ff; 74:16; 136:7ff; 104:19; 148:3) or even as a symbol for God himself (Ps 84:11). On the other hand the Sun is dealt with critically because of the astral cults in the ancient Near East and their influence on Israel. Biblical texts demythologize the Sun (Gn 1:14ff; Ps 19:5) and criticize its worship (Dt 4:19; Ez 8:16; Jer 8:2; Job 31:26ff, cf. 2 Kings 23:5ff). The Sun plays no significant role in descriptions of theophany but its darkening is often mentioned as a sign of the Day of the Lord (Is 13:10; Jl 3:4; Am 8:9).

The latter probably refers to experiences or descriptions of total or nearly total solar eclipses which took place four times in the Near East during the age of the Old Testament: July 31, 1063 B.C.; August 15, 831 B.C., June 15, 763

[57] Ernst Jenni/ Claus Westermann, *Theologisches Handwörterbuch zum Alten Testament I*: col. 987ff.

[58] Karl-Heinrich Bieritz, *Das Kirchenjahr. Feste, Gedenk- und Feiertage in Geschichte und Gegenwart*, (Berlin: Union Verlag, 1988, 2nd ed.), 28.

B.C. and May 18, 585 B.C.[59] But there are no direct references to solar eclipses in the Bible. Obviously the Israelites didn't use them in order to date historical events or mark historical eras like other nations did. This fact would also confirm that they considered them as natural phenomena, not as divine signs. Despite this there are several passages where the choice of words makes clear that the prophets had the image of a solar eclipse in mind (Is 13:10; Ez 32:7; Joel 3:4; Am 8:9, Mi 3:6). Additionally, in some cases the corona of a solar eclipse was described by Israelites and non-Israelites like wings which would explain the widespread symbol of the Sun with wings among the ancients (cf. Mal 3:20).[60] In the end the Old Testament doesn't speak only about the darkening of the Sun but also predicts the end of the Sun and confirms its finitude (Is 60:19).

The New Testament mentions the Sun 32 times and uses the word ἥλιος (= hélios: the Sun, sunlight; Mt 5:46; 13:43; 17:2; Lk 21:25; Acts 2:20; 1 Cor 15:41; Rv 1:16, etc.). Like the Old Testament refers to the cosmic changes on the Day of the Lord there are also such descriptions regarding the Pentecost story (Acts 2:20), the second coming of Christ (Mt 24:29) and the apocalyptical passages (Rv 6:12). In the end the New Jerusalem will not need the Sun any longer because God is its light (Rv 21:23).

## The Moon

יָרֵחַ (=yareach: Moon) occurs 26 times in the Old Testament (e.g. Gn 37:9; Jo 10:12f; Is 13:10; Jr 31:35; Ez 32:7; Joel 2:10; 3:4.15; Pss 8:3; 72:5; 104:19; 121:6; 136:9; 148:3; Job 25:5; Eccl 12:2) and is maybe a derivate of ארח (= to wander). The term is also connected to a name of an astral deity.[61] Moon worship was very popular in ancient times (cf. Is 47:13). The Moon was in charge of fertility and births (because of the menstruation cycle), connected

[59] E. Walter Maunder, ibid., 120f.
[60] Cf. E. Walter Maunder, ibid., 123f.
[61] Wilhelm Gesenius, ibid., 319.

to the underworld and mortuary cults (because of its disappearing during the new moon phases) and seen as a deity responsible for oracles and vows (because of its constant and reliable movements). Mesopotamia was well-known for worshipping the moon-god Sin who was superior even to the sun-god Samas. In Haran there was a big temple of this cult and the Jewish tradition knew that Abram's father Terah (cf. Gn 11:31) had been an enthusiastic worshipper of the moon-god.[62] Later, during the times of the Judges, Sun and Moon were seen as embodiments of Baal and Ashtoreth who reigned as heavenly king and queen.[63] Israel was sometimes also influenced and attracted by these pagan cults (2 Kgs 21:3; 23:4f; Jer 8:2) even if the Torah forbade it expressively (Dt 4:19; 17:3). The first priestly creation story emphasizes that also the Moon was created by God as the lesser light to govern the night and to mark with the other celestial bodies the seasons, days and years (Gn 1:14ff).

The Moon had a high importance for the calendar. Its repeating phases have defined the monthly division of the year. The Israelite year was a lunar year with 12 months of 29 or 30 days, according to the natural lunations.[64] A lunation is the mean time of one lunar phase cycle. In order to reach the length of a solar year it was necessary to add a thirteenth month every 2-3 years. Every new month started with the new Moon which was the moment in the evening when the first crescent became visible after its conjunction with the sun. Today astronomical new Moon means the time of the conjunction itself when the Moon is invisible. The new Moon festivals had special relevance in Israel (Nm 10:10; 28:11ff). The new Moon of the seventh month

---

[62] E. Walter Maunder, ibid., 87. A differentiated article about the Moon worship in the ancient cultures is written by: Gabriele Theuer, *Der Mond*, in: *Das wissenschaftliche Bibellexikon im Internet*, April 2010: http://www.bibelwissenschaft.de/nc/wibilex/das-bibellexikon/details/quelle/WIBI/referenz/27985/cache/f1e54767c88d7b9247677cfa360180dc/ last access: 12 Oktober 2011

[63] E. Walter Maunder, ibid., 89f. The Ashtoreth cult (cf. Ishtar) was later related to the Venus too.

[64] Karl-Heinrich Bieritz, ibid., 40.

was a day off and became a holiday (Lv 23:23ff; Nm 29:1ff). Late Judaism declared this day as New Year's day.

In the New Testament σελήνη (= seléné: moon) is mentioned 9 times, often next to the Sun and the stars (Lk 21:25; 1 Cor 15:41; Rv 6:12f etc.). Like the Old Testament we find also here apocalyptical passages about the darkening of the Moon and its transformation in blood in the Last Days (Mt 24:29; Mk 13:24; Acts 2:20). The red colour is typical of the darkened Moon so that these passages could also be based on observations of lunar eclipses. In the end the light of the Moon as well as the Sun will not be necessary in the New Jerusalem (Rv 21:23).

**The Stars and Constellations**

The word for "star" in the Old Testament is כּוֹכָב (= kokab)[65] which appears 37 times (including 10 times in the phrase כּוֹכְבֵי הַשָּׁמַיִם = kowkbe hashamayim: stars of heaven).[66] The New Testament uses the word ἀστήρ (= aster: a [single] star; e.g. Matthew 2:2ff) 24 times, ἄστρον (= astron: a star [as celestial body], constellation; e.g. Luke 21,25; Acts 7:43; Hebrew 11:12) 24 times and φωστήρ (= phóstér: a light, an illuminator, perhaps the sun; a star; brilliancy; e.g. Phil 2:15) 2 times.[67] Often they were mentioned in one line with the Sun and the Moon and are especially a metaphor for innumerableness (Gn 15:5; 22:17; Dt 1:10; Na 3:16, Heb 11:12). Indeed, "the stars and the heaven, whose host they are, were used by the Hebrew writers to express the superlatives of number, height, and of expanse."[68]

In the Bible the stars are seen as created by God (Gn 1:16; Ps 136:7-9 et al.). He counts their number (Ps 147:4) and knows their names (cf. Is 40:26).

[65] Cf. Wilhelm Gesenius, ibid., 336f.

[66] Ernst Jenni/ Claus Westermann, *Theologisches Handwörterbuch zum Alten Testament II*: col. 968.

[67] Walter Bauer, ibid., col. 233ff, 1725f.

[68] E. Walter Maunder, ibid., 95.

They seem to be lively creatures because they are able to praise God (Ps 148:3) and even fight from heaven (Jgs 5:20). But they are not considered and worshipped as deities like in the neighbouring countries of Israel. They are only "lights" whose task is to shine at night and serve for the division of time (Gn 1:16-18). Although the Torah has clearly forbade the worship of astral deities (Dt 4:19) there was frequently a conflict about it (cf. Am 5:26; 2 Kings 21:5; 23,4ff; Jer 8:2; 19:13; Ez 8:16; Acts 7:43). Connected to worshipping astral deities is astrology which was widely practiced in Babylon (Dn 2:27; 4:4; 5:11) and also rejected in the Bible as pagan practice (but cf. Mt 2:2). Otherwise stars in the Bible are often signs of divine activities and revelations, e.g. of judgements (Ez 32:7) or are involved in apocalyptical events (Mt24:29; Rv 6:13; 8:12; 12:4). They could signify symbolically single persons like in the phrases כּוֹכָב מִיַּעֲקֹב (= kokab mi·yaaqob: Star out of Jacob; Nm 24:17) or denote groups or communities (Dn 12:3; Phil 2:15; cf. Rv 1:16; 2:1; 3:1[69]).

We find the first vague reference in the Bible to the constellations of the zodiac already in the story of Joseph's second dream (Gn 37:9-11). Some exegetes recognize a connection between the twelve tribes of Israel and the twelve constellations of the zodiac. Indeed, the twelve constellations of the Greek zodiac were already known in Mesopotamia, Egypt and Canaan even if their names sometimes differed.[70] The Bible mentions some single stars and constellations by name but their translation or meanings are often unclear:

עָשׁ or עַיִשׁ (=Ash or Ayish; Job 9:9; 38:32) are usually seen as one constellation and rendered as the Great Bear, but also as Aldebaran with

[69] Maybe the seven stars in the book Revelation were originally a constellation, eventually Ursa Major (Greater Bear), Walter Bauer, ibid., col. 234.
[70] E. Walter Maunder, ibid., 186ff.

other stars of the Hyades, Capella and stars of Auriga, the Pleiades or as Arcturus.[71]

Another constellation mentioned in the Bible is כְּסִיל (= Kesil; Job 9:9; 38:32; Am 5:8) which is mostly translated as Orion. The plural of the term seems to signify big constellations in general (Is 13:10).[72]

כִּימָה (= Kimah; Job 9:9; 38:31; Am 5:8) is mostly interpreted as Pleiades but some Old Testament scholars suggest also Scorpio or the single star Sirius.[73]

מַזָּרוֹת (= mazzaroth; Job 38:32; cf. 2 Kings 23:5) is obviously also an astronomical term which was seen as a constellation (Great Bear, Hyades) or as a special star (e.g. morning and evening appearances of Venus) but also generally as the zodiac signs.[74]

לִוְיָתָן (=Livyathan: Leviathan) which means a serpent or great reptile, could also be used on some places in an astronomical sense (e.g. Job 3:8f; Is 27:1). It would refer to one of the stellar dragons like the constellations of Dragon, Hydra or Cetus.[75] Many myths in the ancient world narrate that a dragon devours the Sun or Moon during their eclipses. Indeed a solar or lunar eclipse happens only when the latter is close to two nodes in the constellation of Dragon, called "Dragon's head" and "Dragon's Tail).[76]

*Διόσκουροι* (=Dioskouroi: the Dioscuri, Castor and Pollux; Acts 28:11) is a part of the Gemini constellation and the only one named in the New Testament. In Greek mythology Castor and Pollux were the sons of Zeus and Leda, also being the patrons of sailors.

---

[71] Wilhelm Gesenius, ibid., 625. Cf. the discussion in: E. Walter Maunder, ibid., 258ff.
[72] Wilhelm Gesenius, ibid., 356.
[73] Ibid., 344.
[74] Ibid., 410.
[75] Cf. E. Walter Maunder, ibid., 196ff.
[76] Cf. ibid., 199ff.

## The Planets, Comets and Meteors

The planets are not explicitly mentioned in the Scripture. Possibly the singular Hebrew word מַזָּלוֹת (= mazzaloth; 2 Kgs 23:5) means "planets"[77] but usually it is more generally translated as "constellations".[78] Interesting is also the singular phrase ἀστέρες πλάνῆται (=asteres planétai: wandering stars; Jude 13) which exactly describes the planets as they are considered and named in ancient times. In the New Testament it became a title for false teachers who misled people.

It is known that the ancients counted seven planets (Mercury, Venus, Mars, Jupiter and Saturn) including the Sun and Moon even if they already recognized that the last two were quite different from the other five.[79] But the varying identifications between celestial bodies and astral deities make it difficult to find exact biblical references to the planets. Most likely the astral god כִּיּוּן (=Kiyyun: Kiyyun; based on Akkadian: kaimanu; Am 5:26) which was called in Greek Ῥεμφάν (= Rhemphan: Rephan; Acts 7:43) is identified as the planet Saturn.[80] An interesting observation is that the ancient numbering and naming of the seven planets is connected to the division of seven days per week and their names (e.g. Saturn – Saturday etc.) thereby the Jewish division of a seven-day week was primary in this naming process.[81]

A further biblical reference to a planet is the mention of the "morning star" which refers to the planet Venus (which is astronomically identical with the evening star). The Scripture uses various terms and phrases in order to signify different persons as the morning star: The word הֵילֵל (= helel:

[77] Ibid., 130. Cf. Steward Custer, *The Stars Speak. Astronomy in the Bible*, (Greenville/SC: Bob Jones University Press, 2002, 2nd ed.), 125f.
[78] Wilhelm Gesenius, ibid., 411.
[79] E. Walter Maunder, 130f.
[80] Wilhelm Gesenius, ibid., 343. Cf. Walter Bauer, ibid., col. 233ff, 1461.
[81] Cf. E. Walter Maunder, ibid., 135f.139.

morning star [or moon][82]) signifies the king of Babel as a fallen star (Is 14:12). The phrase ἀστὴρ ὁ πρωϊνός (= aster ho prōinos: morning star, Venus; Rv 22:16; cf. 2,28) denotes Jesus Christ who rises as φωσφόρος (= phósphoros: light-bearing, radiant, the morning-star; 2 Pt 1:19)[83] in our hearts.
Other astronomical phenomena are not exactly identifiable. That biblical passages about falling stars (Dn 8:10; Mk 13:25; Rv 6:13) could refer to comets or meteors are more speculations than assured facts.[84]

### The Ordinances

"In the sublime and ordered movements of the various heavenly bodies, the Hebrews recognized the ordinances of God."[85] Even if in biblical times there was no knowledge of the natural laws behind astronomical phenomena the movements of Sun, Moon and stars were considered as wonderful orders given by God (Ps 148:5-6). These orders were considered as a sign of the immense greatness and wisdom of God (Job 38:31-33)
For instance the movement of the Sun - its predictable rising, continuous course through the sky and setting - inspired the praise of the creator and led to the affirmation that "the law of the Lord is perfect" (Ps 19:4-6). The constant cycle of the moon phases was considered as a continuous governing of the night (Gn 1:16). Thousands of stars observed on a clear night without today's light pollution were seen as starry hosts of heaven which were made, counted and named by God (Ps 147:4; Is 40:26). The planets were recognized as wandering stars which behave differently to the fixed stars. Their strange movements in the sky were obvious even if the backward (retrograde) motion was not explainable at that time.
The earliest observations of order were used for the measuring of time. The rising of the Sun, Moon and stars in the East, their culmination in the South

---

[82] Wilhelm Gesenius, ibid., 179.
[83] Walter Bauer, ibid., col. 234, 1725f
[84] Cf. E. Walter Maunder, ibid., 103ff.
[85] Ibid., 61.

and their setting in the West were well known. Even if the sunset marked the beginning of the calendar day, the sunrise marked the beginning of the work day (Ps 104:22f.). "The thought that each new day, beginning with a new outburst of light, was, in its degree, a kind of new creation, an emblem of the original act by which the world was brought into being, renders appropriate and beautiful the ascription of the term "morning star".[86] Especially, this heliacal rising of the stars played a special role in the division of time and development of the calendar. The first visibility of particular stars and constellations marked the seasons and their durations as well as the length of a year (365 or 366 days). The length of a year could be determined by observing the heliacal rising of a particular body and waiting for its next occurrence.

Whereas the pagan nations worshiped all these celestial bodies as manifestations of deities the Israelites recognized them clearly as created by God and ruled by his ordinances. Even if the stars sometimes seemed to be lively beings representing angelic hosts of heaven (Jgs 5:20; Job 38:7) they were always agents of God and subordinate to him. Nevertheless we have to bear in mind that the Bible didn't describe astronomical observations in a scientific way but in their theological meaning (e.g. Jer 31:35f): "The point of view always taken in Scripture is the theo-centric one; the relation sought to be brought out is not the relation of thing to thing – which is the objective of physical science – but the relation of creature to Creator."[87]

### The astronomical miracles

The latter insight that the Scripture doesn't teach astronomy or physics is also important regarding the miracles which are connected with astronomical phenomena. There are three stories which report extraordinary astronomical

[86] E. Walter Maunder, ibid., 60.
[87] E. Walter Maunder, ibid., 61f.

events: Joshua's long day (Jo 10:12-14), the dial of Ahaz (2 Kings 20:9-11) and the star of Bethlehem (Mt 2:1-12).

The first story (Jo 10:12-14) narrates that on one day the Sun and Moon delayed their setting as the Israelites fought in Canaan against a coalition of five Amorite kings. Joshua recognized during the battle that he couldn't defeat them on one day so he prayed for stopping the Sun and Moon in order to gain more daylight. His prayer was answered and "so the Sun stood still and the Moon stayed in place until the nation of Israel had defeated its enemies" (Jo 10:13). Literally the translation of the phrase is, "The Sun hasted not to go down". From a scientific point of view this event would mean a stopping or deceleration of the rotation of the Earth (whereas at that time the Israelites assumed that the Sun and Moon revolve around the Earth)!
There are several interpretations of the story[88]: A psychological interpretation implies that the Israelites fought so hard against their enemies that they felt like they had worked two days. A meteorological interpretation suggests that the Sun was shadowed by clouds (cf. Jo 10:11) so that the Israelites could fight as if for two days because of the cooler weather (but the enemies would have benefited too!) An astronomical interpretation assumes a solar eclipse but this is not reported for that time and additionally such an event runs only for some minutes not a whole day. Others guessed a certain refraction of light which seems to interrupt the relative motion of the Sun and Moon. Finally, a religio-historical interpretation refers to the sun sanctuary of Gibeon and moon sanctuary of Ajalon so that Joshua's prayer would have stopped the oracles given to the Amorites for their further battle plans. Adding a literary-critical point of view, a later editor forgot or cancelled the Moon in v.13b only emphasizing the lasting sun in the sky so that this miracle became a miracle

[88] Cf. Steward Custer, ibid., 104f. and Donald B. DeYoung, Astronomy and the Bible, (Wimona Lake, IN: BMH Books, 2010), 42.

of nature.[89] This religio-historical interpretation could be supported by the possible translation of the Hebrew words דָּמַם (=damam: cease; cf. Ps 35:15; Lam 2:18) and עָמַד (=amad: stand, stop; cf. 2 Kgs 4:6; Jon 1:15) but it eliminates every direct astronomical cause. However, all these explanations are very speculative and contradict sometimes the intention of the story, especially Joshua's prayer! There is no scientific reason which describes satisfyingly what happened on this special day. The Scripture itself summarized that "there has never been a day like this" (Jo 10:14). Therefore "Joshua's 'long day' cannot be explained as a natural phenomenon but must be interpreted as a supernatural miracle."[90]

The second story (2 Kgs 20:9-11; cf. Is 38:1-7) narrates that the time even ran backwards! The sick king Hezekiah asked for this outstanding sign as a proof that God fulfils his promises to heal him. After a prayer of the prophet Isaiah the shadow of the Sun moved 10 steps backwards. From a scientific point of view this event would mean that God reversed the rotation of the earth so that the Sun moved seemingly toward the East again instead of toward the West! It is interesting that the Bible mentions here one of the oldest astronomical instruments: the sun dial of Ahaz (2 Kings 20:9ff; Is 38:8) which was a stairway in the royal palace[91] or a large obelisk surrounded by steps which acted as the gnomon.[92] However, this miracle is also not explainable by scientific reasons even if it probably had only local instead of worldwide effects (cf. 2 Chr 32:31). Widely circulating reports about computers which had supposedly found the long days of Joshua and

---

[89] J. Conrad et. al, *Das Alte Testament mit Erklärungen 1*, (Berlin: Evangelische Haupt-Bibelgesellschaft, 1982), 372f.
[90] Steward Custer, ibid., 104.
[91] G. Fohrer in: Ernst Jenni/ Claus Westermann, *Theologisches Handwörterbuch zum Alten Testament II*: col. 995.
[92] Steward Custer, ibid., 104f.

Hezekiah are unsubstantiated. "Neither NASA nor any other space agency confirms the urban legend of missing time."[93]

The third story of an astronomical miracle is about the star of Bethlehem which guided the wise men to the new born Messiah (Mt 2:1-12). They saw the star ἐν τῇ ἀνατολῇ (= en tē anatolē) which means "in its rising" or "star in the East" (Mt 2:2). Many scholars tried to identify this star with astronomical objects or phenomena. A first explanation which is often artistically depicted is a suddenly emerging comet. But there is no knowledge of bright comets around the time of Christ's birth, except 44 B.C. and 17 B.C. and 66 A.D.[94] The closest to the time is Halley's Comet appearing in 11 B.C. which would be 4-7 years before the birth of Jesus Christ. Comets were seen as harbingers of great historical events but mostly of negative happenings and catastrophes. A second suggestion is the identification of the star with a seldom planetary conjunction of Jupiter and Saturn in 7 B.C. In 1603/04 Johannes Kepler calculated this conjunction, and in 1925 the East German professor of ancient oriental studies Paul Schnabel (1887-1947) found a reference to this conjunction in a Neo-Babylonian cuneiform tablet, known as the Star Calendar of Sippar.[95] That in ancient times Jupiter was usually considered as the star of kings and Saturn as the star of the Hebrews would also fit to the search of the wise men for a newborn king of the Jews. But the story mentions only one star and additionally the conjunction of Jupiter and Saturn takes place periodically[96] (there was also an even closer conjunction of both planets in 66 B.C.[97]). A third explanation is linked to a supernova

---

[93] Donald B. DeYoung, ibid., 43.
[94] Werner Gitt, *Signale aus dem All. Wozu gibt es Sterne*, (Bielefeld: CLV Verlag, 2004, 4th ed.), 113.
[95] Ibid., 115.
[96] Ibid., 114, footnote 29: Simple Jupiter-Saturn-Conjunctions take place every 20 years, threefold conjunctions in different constellations every 258 years, threefold conjunctions in one constellation every 774 years. (The last one was on 15 August and 11 October, 1940 and on 20 February 1941 in the constellation of Aries.)
[97] Donald B. DeYoung, ibid., 56.

which is a burst of a dying, instable star but there is no historical report of such a unique astronomical event at that time. The closest reports date from 134 B.C. and 173 A.D.[98] All these conjectures do not make comprehensible how a comet, star or planets and also a supernova which move on the night sky from East to West can show the way to a particular place or house on earth. Additionally, Herod and his counsellors didn't notice any salient astronomical events before the wise men arrived. Whatever the wise men observed in the night sky during their journey they have needed an inner epiphany (and also the advice of the prophetical scriptures given by Herod's counsellors!) in order to find the way to the newborn Christ, who should be the promised star out of the house of Jacob (Nm 24:17). The result is "that the Star of Bethlehem cannot be explained by natural phenomena.... The great mystery of the first Christmas is not the identification of the Star of Bethlehem. It is the question of why the Magi were chosen to follow the light of the Messiah, and why we are given the same invitation today."[99]

The investigation of these three miracles seems to be sobering in view of astronomical insights in the Bible. Obviously the dialogue between theology and natural science cannot have the goal to find scientific explanations for miraculous stories in the Bible. For instance, the astronomical miracles in the Bible were always unique but natural science is based on repeatable observations and experiments. In every case the Scripture is not focused on astronomical phenomena as such nor has a scientific interest in them. Furthermore the various experiences of nature, including the observation of celestial bodies are always connected to a spiritual message or theological statement in order to confess that "the sun, moon, and stars readily obey the Creator who placed them in the sky by the power of His Word"[100] or according

[98] Werner Gitt, ibid., 114.
[99] Donald B. DeYoung, ibid., 57.
[100] Ibid., 43.

to the Christmas story that "the love born in this humble place is the love that moves the sun and the stars."[101] This means not that these stories are based only on delusions without any real astronomical-explanations. To the contrary! Especially "the wise men confirm the church's conviction... that we should believe that God's existence is in principal open to rational demonstrations... That (they) find their way to Jesus by the sign of a star should, therefore, not be surprising. But it is also the case that this 'natural knowledge' requires narration through the stories that have been given us in scripture."[102] This biblical encounter between natural knowledge and stories of faith mark the meeting point of Theology and natural science.

[101] Stanley Hauerwas, *Brazos Theological Commentary on The Bible – Matthew*, (Grand Rapids, MI: Brazos Press, 2009, 2nd ed.), 39.
[102] Stanley Hauerwas, *Brazos Theological Commentary on The Bible – Matthew*: 39.

# CHAPTER FOUR
# SYSTEMATIC – THEOLOGICAL REFLECTION

## Impulses from a Theology of Creation

We encounter the first mention of the celestial bodies when the Scripture speaks about creation. The fact that there are two different creation stories (Gn 1:1-2:4a and Gn 2:4b-4:2) which stand side by side in the Scripture is already an important indicator for the dialogue between theology and natural science. It shows that the conceptions of the world were always changing. There is no the 'biblical' or 'Christian' conception of the world but every generation has to formulate their own creed using the best knowledge of their time. The belief in God as creator is not bound to a particular (scientific) concept of the world. Otherwise natural science also has to recognize that knowledge is changing and that there is not 'the' scientific concept of the world. In the last case science would become a substitute for religion or philosophy.

The first biblical creation story with the astronomical references (Gn.1:1-2:4a) doesn't present a scientific doctrine about the genesis of the universe but seeks to confess primarily the God of Israel as its only creator. It was written between 550-450 B.C. during the Babylonian Exile (587-538 B.C.) as a response to the surrounding pagan religion which worshipped the celestial bodies as astral deities. The priestly writers struggled with this religious environment and formulated their own genuine creed using the knowledge of their time. The Babylonian Exile made a realignment regarding nature, especially regarding the celestial bodies, very necessary, particularly since the Israelites were forced to worship them too. Additionally it is important to recognize that this creation story was written after the people of Israel had already experienced God's liberating actions long before (e.g. the Exodus) so that the belief in God as creator of nature is historically subordinated to the belief in God as liberator. Originally Israel understood 'creation' as primarily defined by God's actions throughout history (cf. Ps 66:1-7; 77:12-21) rather than in natural processes. Maybe here is a source of the doctrine of *continuous creation*, originally describing God's creating action in history and then in nature. It claims that "God is present in the evolutionary process – not as its sole determinant...but as the source and guide of its fruitfulness. The work of the creator continues, not least throughout the natural processes that are expressions of God's will."[103] The sustaining orders but also the preservation of the creation could be explained by this doctrine. When theologians enters the dialogue with natural science they have to keep in mind that both beliefs in God as acting in nature as well as acting in history belong together and that He is continuously creating in both areas.

Furthermore it is important to recognize that "the doctrine of creation is not concerned with temporal origin but with ontological origin. It is proposed as the answer to the question of why anything exists at all, and not to the question of how it all began."[104] Indeed, a careful reading and interpretation of the first creation story can help to overcome barriers and support the dialogue between theology and natural science. The translation and interpretation of the phrase בְּרֵשִׁית (=bə·rešit: in the beginning; Gn 1:1) have wide-ranging consequences, depending on understanding it as a moment of time or as a term for source and origin (so e.g. Ps 111:10; cf. John 1:1). The temporal interpretation has the problem of dating the creation (although time is a category starting after creation!) and its period of seven "days" (which cannot be defined before the sun was created on the fourth day!) and has to bring them in accordance with the complex physical processes at the beginning of the universe. Therefore it is more appropriate to interpret "beginning" in a

[103] John Polkinghorne, *Science and Theology: An Introduction*, (Minneapolis, MN: Fortress Press, 1998), 80.
[104] Ibid., 79f.

substantive sense in order to avoid a false contradiction between creation and science and facilitate a fruitful connection between faith and reason. Such a theological reading "helps us focus on the divine purpose for creation rather than on physical processes that gave rise to the created world."[105] Additionally, "a clear distinction between 'beginning' as first instance in an unfolding process and 'beginning' as ultimate source and purpose helps us to see, materialism is neither entailed by nor part of modern scientific cosmology" and let Christian faith be "well prepared to endorse modern science while rejecting the faux metaphysics of modern scientism."[106]

An important feature of the first biblical creation story is the emphasis on the sovereignty of God as creator and the consequential demythologizing of the Babylonian conception of the world. In the beginning God is the only creator of everything. Heaven and earth are not made by the struggle of chaotic divine powers like the non-Israeli mythologies narrated[107] but God alone created (בָּרָא = bara: create, make – only used regarding God!) them by speaking his sovereign word so that they came into existence. The creation by the divine word distinguishes clearly creator from the world but otherwise it also expresses that both are related to one another. Neither the creation is divine nor is it an emanation of the creator, which speaks against pantheism. The fact that the celestial bodies are not deities any longer provides an interesting access to dialogue between theology and natural science: the biblical belief in God as creator which includes the demythologizing of the

[105] Cf. R.R. Reno, *Brazos Theological Commentary on The Bible – Genesis*, (Grand Rapids, MI: Brazos Press, 2010), 29ff

[106] Ibid., 35. Reno hints at the "Modern Atheism" represented e.g. by Richard Dawkins, *The Blind Watchmaker*, (New York: Penguin, 1990).

[107] See e.g. references in Gn 1:2 to תהום (= tehom: deep, sea, abyss) which is connected to the Babylonian chaos dragon Tiamat, or בהו (= bohu: emptiness) which is linked to the nocturnal mother goddess Baau). The Babylonian creation myth Enûma Eliš describes the creation of the world by the struggle of the Babylonian deity Marduk against the dragon Tiamat. In the following the latter one was divided and became heaven and earth. Cf. Gerhard von Rad, *Das erste Buch Mose, ATD 2*, (Göttingen: Vandenhoek & Ruprecht, 1949), 38.

world can be described as an important step toward developing natural science at all. Only after the Sun, Moon and stars were no longer objects of worship but objects made by God they could be described and explored as natural things. The demythologizing of the celestial bodies as “lamps” started the division of astronomy from astrology and laid the foundation for their later scientific examination. Looked at in that light there is a link between the de-deification of the celestial bodies in the first biblical creation story and the landing on the moon in the last century![108] Therefore some theologians claim that the Judeo-Christian belief in God as creator who is distinguished from the world was an enablement of the later natural science.[109] So the belief in God as creator is not a contradiction to natural science but furthermore enabled it!

As already mentioned there are a lot astronomical references in poetic texts, like the Psalms (Pss 8; 19; 104; 147; 148 etc.). They praise the work of God in history and nature. People thank God who liberates his people, and at the same time he guides the Sun, Moon and stars according to his ordinances. Only the form of the texts makes clear that they present not scientific descriptions or factual knowledge because the authors often speak metaphorically. This kind of nature poetry has its own worth and may not be measured by scientific standards. A dialogue with science has to indicate that this is a legitimate expression of human experience of nature like other arts. These experiences and descriptions of nature belong to our culture and enrich the lives of individuals. The scientific approach is not the only one which describes our world adequately but needs to be complemented by others. "The task is to accept the scientific story at its own level but to

[108] Cf. Claus Westermann, *Schöpfung*, (Stuttgart: Kreuz-Verlag, 1983), 64.
[109] Hans Küng, *Der Anfang aller Dinge. Naturwissenschaft und Religion*, (München: Piper Verlag, 2008), 141.

propose an alternative meta-interpretation of that story, read out from the belief that behind it lie the creative purposes of God."[110]

We find further astronomical references in the wisdom literature, especially in the book of Job (9:1-11; 14:1-6; 22:12ff, 25:1-6; 38:31-33). Here these references serve the deep theological reflection considering the human experiences of suffering and death. Dealing with subjects of astronomy leads easily to deep questions about the meaning of life but also the problem of theodicy. We find this connection already in the book of Deutero-Isaiah (Is 40-55) when he tried to comfort his people during the Babylonian captivity and to strengthen their faith in God's releasing power by lifting up their eyes to the stars in the night sky (Is 40:26-31). Thus astronomical references in these contexts do not have an end in themselves but function as pastoral care for individuals or even for a whole people. It is typical that thoughts of the creation often arise in the Scripture in connection with experiences of hardship and liberation, whereby the belief in God as liberator preceded the belief in God as creator! However, a dialogue with science needs to address the question of the meaning of life and cannot neglect the problem of evil and human suffering in the world. Together we need to discuss our responsibility for the conditions of life on our planet and how we can make them better. Additionally, a dialogue always happens between real people who could be affected existentially by these questions.

In the time between the Testaments we encounter initially the doctrine of *creation ex nihilo* (2 Mc 7:28), typically also in the context of the strengthening of faith in times of persecution and hardship. Originally the biblical creation stories didn't include this doctrine explicitly because God didn't create the cosmos out of nothing but formed it out of primal matter. In the priestly

---

[110] John Polkinghorne, *Science and Theology:* 77.

creation story the creation by God means more separating of the elements, bringing order in the chaos, dividing space and time, and naming the created things. This aspect of order and ordinances and how we live in accordance with these can be a fruitful subject of the dialogue too. Nevertheless, the doctrine of *creation ex nihilo* is a quite necessary consequence of the biblical witness of the creation by God. It secures on the one hand the divinity of God and claims on the other hand the createdness of all things. Nothing but God is God, which interestingly is also the historical background of the struggle against idolatry in 2 Mc 7:28. "There is nothing (*nihil*) other than the one true God and the set of all things he made.... Idolatry is loyalty to *nihil*, a devotion to the lifeless, empty abyss of death, which is the antithesis of the future promised in the covenant. This is why idolatry is the mother of all sins in the Old Testament and also why St. Paul makes idolatry the fundamental, original sin in Rom.1."[111] From this point of view it is also clear why the Scripture negates every divinization of nature and its laws, including the celestial bodies and their orders (cf. the different worldview of Astrology). Additionally, the doctrine of *creation ex nihilo* sharpens our understanding of God's relation to the world: It "formulates God's transcendence in terms of uniqueness rather than supremacy or difference, what makes God divine is consistent with his immediacy and presence to finite reality. God leaves nothing behind. There is no divine reality other than the singular LORD, and therefore the neither betrays nor contradicts his divinity by drawing near."[112] This is important for the dialogue between Theology and natural science, especially when we discuss the question of God and His presence in the universe and our world.

[111] R.R. Reno, ibid., 40f.
[112] R.R. Reno, ibid., 42.

## The Importance of a Trinitarian Approach

First, it is necessary to emphasize that the New Testament holds to the belief in God as the one creator of the universe (e.g. Acts 17:24) in distinction to various heresies (e.g. Gnosticism), who denied a creation by the one true God. Paul even claims that all human beings could recognize the work of God in His creation (Rom 1:20) and that the creation is involved in God's further salvation (Rom 8:20-21). A specific Christian theology of creation doesn't contradict Old Testament concepts about the protological creation but interprets them new by a messianic and eschatological view. A "Christian understanding proclaims the creator of heaven and earth as 'the Father of Jesus Christ', and develops Old Testament monotheism in a Trinitarian sense: the Father created heaven and earth through the Son in the Spirit."[113] The Christian doctrine of creation is defined by God's revelation in Jesus Christ as the redeemer of human beings as well as of the whole cosmos. "If he is the ground of salvation for the whole creation..., he is then also the ground for the existence of the whole creation, human beings and nature alike."[114] There is a parallel between the Old and New Testaments in the perception of God: in the Old Testament God is perceived first as liberator (Exodus) and then as creator. In the New Testament Jesus Christ is recognized first as redeemer and then as co-creator and mediator in the protological creation (John 1:1-3; 1 Cor 8:6; Co 1:15-17). "The awareness of the universality of salvation in and through Christ leads to the insight that 'in him all things were created' (Eph 1:9; Col 1:15ff)"[115] but also sustained and preserved (Heb 1:2f.). The re-discovering of the belief in the Cosmic Christ avoids an anthropological narrowing and will be a helpful theological base for the dialogue between theology and science, especially astronomy.

---

[113] Jürgen Moltmann, *God in Creation: A New Theology of Creation and the Spirit of God*, (Minneapolis, MN: Fortress Press, 1993), 94.
[114] Ibid., 94
[115] Ibid., 95.

"Without a pneumatological doctrine of creation there cannot be a Christian doctrine of creation at all."[116] The third person of the Trinity is involved in the protological creation like the Father and the Son. In the Old Testament the Spirit is already mentioned in the first creation story (Gn 1:2) and furthermore understood as the divine power by which everything is made and as giver of life (e.g. Ps 104:29f.; Ez 37). In the New Testament the Spirit is connected to eschatological experiences of salvation. It is the earnest of the future glory (2 Cor 1:22; 5:5; Eph. 1:14) which includes the eternal life of individuals as well as the new creation. "The experience of the eschatological reality of the Spirit leads to the conclusion that this is the same Spirit in whose power the Father, through the Son, has created the world, and preserves it."[117] Furthermore the gift of the Spirit represents a new presence of God *in* His creation: "Through his Spirit the Creator is himself involved in his creation."[118] In this sense the Spirit signifies God's immanent creational activity rather than His transcendence. The cosmic Spirit operates in nature as principle of creativity enabling new possibilities and evolution, as holistic principle supporting mutuality and co-operation, and as principle of openness directing toward future and hope.[119] When the cosmic Spirit acts in that way "the universe cannot be viewed as a closed system. It has to be understood as a system that is open – open for God and for his future."[120] This is an important aspect for the dialogue between theology and science.

A specific Christian doctrine of creation is characterized by a Trinitarian approach which balances God's immanence and transcendence. Neither deism emphasizing God's transcendence nor pantheism stressing His immanence coincide with the Christian understanding of creation and

---

[116] Ibid., 99.
[117] Ibid., 96.
[118] Ibid., 97.
[119] Ibid., 100.
[120] Ibid., 103.

therefore cannot be an appropriate theological base for the dialogue between theology and natural science. An option seems to be panentheism but in the end only a Trinitarian approach to the doctrine of creation can really relate God's transcendence with his immanent activity in the creation.[121] Obviously Trinitarian thinking best enables a complementary understanding of the triune God and His activity in the world. This is very important for the dialogue between theology and natural science, e.g. regarding defining reality. Additionally, the Trinity offers two further important insights which affect both theologians and scientists.[122] The first insight is the relational nature of being. It replaced the classical Greek notion of a static being of God by a more dynamic understanding of the Triune God, expressed by the term *perichoresis*. In view of the immanent or essential Trinity it refers to the mutual interpenetration and indwelling of God the Father, the Son and the Holy Spirit who realize an intimate fellowship and eternal community of love. The *perichoresis* is also a model of the interconnectedness and the relational character of the creation. "Modern science encourages the use of relational concepts in its account of physical reality. The Newtonian picture of unchanging individual atoms colliding in the fixed container of pre-existing space has been replaced by Einstein's relativistic insight that space, time and matter are all interlinked, by quantum theory's togetherness-in-separation... and by the idea that all apparently individual electrons are actually excitations of energy in a common quantum field."[123] Furthermore, the dialogue between theology and natural science itself could be anchored in the idea of *perichoresis* which offers "a model of social communion for the world" and calls for a society which is characterized by fundamental interconnectedness with one another, equal participation of everybody, fair communication and

[121] Ibid., 98.103.
[122] Cf. John Polkinghorne, *Science and Theology*: 113.
[123] Ibid., 114.

just relationships.[124] This hermeneutical approach would signify the dialogue between religion and natural science as a consequence of the inner-Trinitarian communion and conversation inviting to a fair discourse between both sides, enabling a complementary view of reality and motivating a discussion of the ethical, social and ecological responsibilities of natural science and research.

It is obvious that the inner-Trinitarian *perichoresis* also affects the economic Trinity which describes how the threefold God is experienced in the history of creation. Thus a second Trinitarian insight derives from the observation that today's "discussions moved away from the kind of metaphysical speculations that were part of thinking in the later patristic period, turning back again to closer linkage with experience."[125] It is the view 'from below' explaining the experiences of the Trinity in our world. According to a Methodist theology experience plays an important role next to the Scripture, tradition and reason. Therefore the dialogue between religion and science cannot abandon talking about experiences of God in our postmodern secular world. Trinitarian theology in this context has to develop "an insightful understanding of how God's activity in creation (the Father's holding of the universe in being), in redemption (the Son's sharing of humanity that we might share in divinity), and in sanctification (the transforming power of the Holy Spirit at work in human lives from within), come together as acts of the one true God whose essence as Love is expressed in mutual interchange between the Persons of the Godhead."[126]

## Eschatological References

The astronomical references in the Bible were often linked to passages about the future which God has promised. The celestial bodies herald the

---

[124] Daniel E. Groody, *Globalization, Spirituality, and Justice*, (New York, NY: Maryknoll, 2010), 62.
[125] John Polkinghorne, *Science and Theology:* 114.
[126] Ibid.

eschatological changes or are affected by them. The biblical belief in God who has created heaven and earth includes necessarily also the belief in their consummation. The Scripture claims the meaningfulness of the universe and of everything what exists and happens in it. Especially the New Testament proclaims the hope in a new creation beyond the end of the current world which was already anticipated in the resurrection of Jesus Christ. It will embrace human beings as well as the whole creation (2 Cor 5:17-18a; Rom 8:18-25; Rv 21:1-5). A dialogue between faith and science is challenged by the fact that the human race will die out and the universe as we know it will end. It is a common notion of theology and science that everything that exists is limited in time and will at some time end. Not only human lives and the history of the human race will be finished at some point but also the existence of the planet Earth, of the celestial bodies like the Sun and the Moon, and of the universe as a whole. Astronomers forecast the end of the Sun's main lifetime in approximately 10 billion years and of the universe perhaps in several hundred billions years. They are not sure yet if the universe will continue to expand forever and decay in low radiation, or if the expansion will come to a standstill and start contracting, finishing in a 'big crunch'. However, the dialogue needs to take seriously these scientific facts and to raise the question of what the end of life and of the universe means. Is the physicist and cosmologist Steven Weinberg right when he claimed, "the more the universe seems comprehensible, the more it also seems pointless".[127] It is necessary to insist that such assertions of meaning or futility of the universe are always philosophical or theological statements. Natural science itself is limited to scientific methods and descriptions of the immanent world. Otherwise theological doctrines of the last things cannot take the place of scientific theories regarding cosmology.

---

[127] Steven Weinberg, *The Fist Three Minutes*, (New York: Pantheon, 1977), 144.

Astronomical references in the Bible are often connected to subjects about the future of the cosmos. They support avoiding an anthropological narrowing of eschatology and broaden the horizon of hope. Christian faith states not only the salvation of individual human beings but proclaims a new creation which includes the whole Earth with all living beings as well as lifeless matter and the whole universe (Col 1:20). "In fact, the matter of new creation...must be God's destiny for the futility-generating (entropy-increasing) matter of this world."[128] Thereby it is important to recognize that "the new creation arises 'out of the old' and not through a divine wiping of the cosmic slate clean for a second attempt at creation 'out of nothing'."[129] This insight contradicts a fatalistic fundamentalism abandoning the world to its complete destruction. Furthermore the old creation will be transformed in a new one which includes continuity as well as discontinuity. The resurrection of Christ is a model for this transformation because "the empty tomb asserts that Christ's risen and glorified body is the transformation of his dead body, thereby implying a destiny in Christ for matter as well as for humanity."[130]

The hope in human destiny beyond death "resides in the faithfulness of a Creator who will not allow the creatures that are the subjects of the divine love simply to fall into nothingness.... God will remember and reconstitute the pattern that is a human being, in an act of resurrection taking place beyond present history."[131] (cf. Mk 12:27). This Christian hope includes the belief in a bodily resurrection, not only the survival of the soul as the immortal essence of a human being. It will be not only an act of revival of the old but a new creating activity of God. Thus this resurrected body will be a new body which is different from the mortal body we have now. "If the resurrected life is to be a true fulfilment, and not just a repeat of an ultimately futile history, the bodies

[128] John Polkinghorne, *Science and Theology:* 116.
[129] Ibid.
[130] Ibid., 117.
[131] Ibid., 115.

of that world-to-come must be different, for they will be everlasting redeemed from mortality."[132] Whereas astronomical references are very seldom connected to human destiny beyond death, 1Cor 15:40-42 is a link to the otherness of the resurrection and the new corporeality: *"There are also heavenly bodies and there are earthly bodies; but the splendor of the heavenly bodies is one kind, and the splendor of the earthly bodies is another. The sun has one kind of splendor, the moon another and the stars another; and star differs from star in splendor. So will it be with the resurrection of the dead... ."* Dealing with astronomical subjects can lead to a dialogue about meaning and destiny of human life without being focused only on the salvation of human beings. It helps to raise the question of human destiny in the context of the new creation of the whole universe. It reveals the Creator's purposes regarding creation and new creation in a two step process: "first a creation separate from God (allowed to make itself, as we thought theologically about an evolutionary universe), with the inevitable mortality that is the necessary cost of new life; then a new creation that is the transformation of the old and not its abolition, and which is not subject to mortality since it is no longer separated from God but integrated into the divine life ('theosis')."[133]

It is obvious that astronomical and cosmological subjects challenge Christian eschatology. If the future, as described in science and theology, affects the present then we have to ask for the consequences for human actions today. In a Christian perspective the goal must be to instruct people about acting in hope. A systematic reflection of what new creation means has to deal today with the myth of human progress and ethics in the light of the environmental

---

[132] Ibid., 116.
[133] Ibid.

crisis.[134] Despite the pessimism of the scientific scenarios regarding life on earth and the future of the universe, our time is influenced by widespread optimistic images of science and technology. Our western culture is shaped by "the metanarrative of the utopian myth of human progress, that is, the belief that science, technology and education will lead us to a perfect and morally better world."[135] Even if political and social utopian myths plunged into a crisis by the last World Wars and the downfall of Communism in the last century, the belief in the scientific and technological progress still persists.

An example for a physical eschatology which transfers the myth of human progress is Frank Tipler's *Physics of Immortality*.[136] He views human beings in a very reductionist manner: as a biochemical machine and the brain as a computer where its programs run.[137] Human life becomes equated with intelligent information processing which will go on even if a human being or the whole human race would die. In the latter case this information process would find other beings or objects to perpetuate it till the universe collapses and finds its final cosmic state, called 'Omega'. The 'Omega Point' is defined as the sum of all information in the Universe, as the completion of all finite existence, and in the end as the embodiment of a physical god.[138] It has the capacity to provide resurrection for individuals by recalling their information. At least Tipler states that theology is only a part of physics and nothing but physical cosmology which is based on the conviction of the immortality of life.[139] This approach is highly speculative regarding its cosmological assumptions and its philosophical implications[140]. Tipler's claim of a

---

[134] Cf. David Wilkinson, *Christian Eschatology and the Physical Universe*, (London: T&T Clark Int'l, 2010), 177ff.

[135] Ibid., 178.

[136] Frank J. Tipler, *The Physics of Immortality*, (New York: Doublesday, 1994); I read and cite the German translation: Frank J. Tipler, *Die Physik der Unsterblichkeit. Moderne Kosmologie, Gott und Auferstehung der Toten*, (München: R.Piper GmbH & Co. KG, 1994)

[137] Ibid., 24.

[138] Ibid., 37.

[139] Ibid., 26, 35, 42.

[140] Arguments against Tipler you find e.g. in: John Polkinghorne, *Science and Theology:* 117 and David Wilkinson, ibid., 20.

"resurrection from the hard disk" looks like a "religious consecration of the human progress"[141] and is an "attempt to give a scientific basis for hope."[142] However, Tipler's reproach is true that theology is often not interested in dialogue with modern science (and vice versa).[143] But the result cannot be the assimilation of theology into physics. Christian eschatology differs greatly from the utopian myth of human progress which trusts in science and technology in order to survive. It is instead based on the belief in the new creation and a bodily resurrection which the transcendent Creator God will provide. "The resurrection faith is not faith in future but in the God of the future."[144] Christian eschatology rejects the myth of human progress by biblical narratives about God's future for the Universe.[145] On the one hand it has to bring together these narratives with modern cosmologies about the end of the universe in order to ground the Christian hope and take seriously the discontinuity of the new creation. On the other hand it has to emphasize, that only the belief in a transcendent God can be the reason for founded hope. Narrative expressed hope will help to deal with the chaotic world, give it meaning and widen our imagination of God's preferred future of the universe.

Furthermore, the biblical narratives about new creation in its personal and cosmic perspectives call to responsible action in the present, especially in times of environmental crisis. Eschatology is an essential motivation for Christian ethics next to the creational approach to ethics. "Eschatological ethics need to be in close relationship with creation ethics" because "our stewardship stems not only from an orientation to the responsibility given in

[141] Hans Dieter Mutschler, *Physik und Christentum – Auferstehung von der Festplatte: Religiöse Weihe für den Fortschritt. Zu Frank Tiplers Buch "Die Physik der Unsterblichkeit"*, in: Publik-Forum 12/1994, (Oberursel: Public-Forum Verlagsgesellschaft mbH: 1994), 45f.
[142] David Wilkinson, ibid., 178.
[143] Frank J. Tipler, ibid., 28-31.
[144] David Wilkinson, ibid., 179.
[145] Ibid., 178f.

Eden but also from an orientation of what God's purposes for the future will be."[146] Christian ethics is always in tension between the 'already' of the creation and the 'not yet' of the new creation. "The tension between continuity and discontinuity in the biblical accounts of resurrection can helpfully form a tension in considering ethics in the future of the Universe. That is, any progress in science either in its impact on the environment or the wider Universe needs to reflect the goodness of creation as gift with the action of God of bringing in new creation."[147]

[146] Ibid., 180.
[147] Ibid., 182.

# CHAPTER FIVE
# THEOLOGY IN THE CONTEXT OF SCIENCE

## Christian Faith Meets Natural Science

If theology takes seriously its context in the western world, then today it needs to be also a "theology in the context of science" and "should be treated as another form of contextual theology".[148] The present chapter discusses the relationship between theology and natural science focused on subjects which are connected to astronomy and cosmology. The following sections will focus primarily on the theology of Wolfhart Pannenberg who was a passionate pioneer of the dialogue between theology and natural science. His approach is insofar an instructive example because it includes very useful but also mistaken arguments we can learn from.

First, it is necessary to analyse the history of the relationship between theology and natural science – a relationship which is very ambivalent. In mediaeval times the monasteries were often centres not only of religious life and theology but also schools of natural sciences and arts. In our context it is noteworthy that monasteries accumulated and recorded astronomical knowledge especially for practical purposes (calendar, agriculture, church architecture) and in some cases even operated their own astronomical observatories. During that time even women like the nuns Hildegard of Bingen and Gertrud of Helfta dealt with astronomy and developed a cosmic spirituality. In the modern era when the conflicts between theology and natural science arose most of the discoverers were nevertheless devout Christians. Today we often face in the media "modern myths" about scientists like Galileo or Copernicus only seen in conflict with the church but "the truth is altogether more complex and correspondingly more interesting."[149] To contemplate these historical facts and narrate these stories in their complexity

---

[148] John Polkinghorne, *Theology in the Context of Science*, (London: SPCK, 2008), xiii.
[149] Cf. John Polkinghorne, *Science and* Theology: 4ff.

could create fruitful dialogue. It is a pity that in the former communist era (in East Germany) till today the relationship between theology and science has been described as predominately negative and antagonistic. Nevertheless, we have to take seriously the given public opinion about the relationship between theology and natural science which is predominately characterized by conflicts between both sides.

In Pannenberg's historical analysis, the process of drifting apart was triggered by the heliocentric world view of Copernicus and its rejection by the catholic and protestant churches. On the other hand it was propelled by the influence of Descartes' principle of inertia (which described mechanistically all changes in the world as influences of bodies on each other so that a bodiless God couldn't be active in the world), the critique of miracles by English deism and the German theology of the Enlightenment (including the historical-critical exegesis), and in the end by the Darwinian theory of evolution.[150] Apart from few exceptions in the Anglo-Saxon theology of the 19th century and the work of Pierre Teilhard de Chardin[151], Pannenberg concludes that "the history of modern natural science to a great deal has been a history of emancipation of science from theological presuppositions.... In modern times, however, theology has been expelled from physics step by step" so that the history of their relationship looks like a "chain of defeats of theological apologetics by the natural science".[152] This conflict since the modern era had lead to a growing alienation and mutual ignorance so that in the last one hundred years theology dealt either with the gaps of natural science or has withdrawn completely from an open discussion. It bothered mostly with the inner religious life or the exegesis of the Scripture and churchly doctrines. For

---

150 Wolfhart Pannenberg, *God and Nature. On the History of the Debates Between Theology and Natural Science*, in: id., *Toward a Theology of Nature: Essays on Science and Faith*, (Louisville, KT: Westminster/John Knox Press, 1993), 52-58.
151 Cf. Wolfhart Pannenberg, *God and* Nature: 51-56f.
152 Wolfhart Pannenberg, *Contingency and Natural Law*, in: id., *Toward a Theology of Nature: Essays on Science and Faith*, (Louisville, KT: Westminster/John Knox Press, 1993), 73.

instance, the very influential dialectical theology (e.g. of Karl Barth) denied any references to scientific insights and methods in their doctrine of creation and saw no necessity for dialogue.[153] Theology should deal only with God's revelation by His Word, and was seen as generally separated from natural science which was considered as human activity belonging to the area of culture. Pannenberg criticized this withdrawal of theology because it has also led to its self-marginalization: The "protection from critique by the natural sciences signifies at the same time the irrelevancy of theological statements, not only for the work of the natural scientist but also for the world view of today's humanity which is rightfully informed by the results of the natural sciences."[154] He complained about such broad theological ignorance regarding natural science and even claimed that this attitude would hurt the divinity of God![155]

According to Pannenberg, the alternative can be only a new "Theology of Nature" which deals with methods and contents of the natural sciences and seeks accordance between Christian faith and the scientific worldview. The "Theology of Nature" is different from the previous natural theology because it presupposed nothing regarding the knowledge of God in nature. It is also not to be equated with a theology of creation which could also be formulated without a connection to natural science. Furthermore Pannenberg warns that "theology must not become pray to the all too comfortable escape to the idea of creation on a special or exclusively theological level which is inaccessible to any critique by the natural sciences."[156] Only a new "Theology of Nature" which grapples with this critique enables a sincere dialogue between both sides based on the belief that "exactly that nature which is researched by

[153] Wolfhart Pannenberg, *God and* Nature: 50.
[154] Wolfhart Pannenberg, *Contingency and Natural Law*: 74.
[155] Cf. the Tuscany Talks in 1996 published in: Dürr, Meyer-Abich, Mutschler, Pannenberg, Wuketits, *Gott, der Mensch und die Wissenschaft*, (Augsburg: Pattloch Verlag, 1997), 106.
[156] Wolfhart Pannenberg, *Contingency and Natural Law*: 74.

natural science would have to be claimed by theology as the creation of God."[157] A doctrine of creation based only on a theological level or on the belief that every individual is created by God would not be enough. "The conviction that God has created 'me' cannot serve as a foundation of a doctrine of creation that is sure in itself" because "the affirmation of divine reality, rather, can be justified only on the condition that the affirmed reality can be understood as the origin of all that is real, that is, also of nature and its possible consummation."[158] Pannenberg refers to the priestly creation story in Gn 1 and states that also the people of Israel could only express their belief in the creator of heaven and earth by using the scientific insights of their time which were provided by Babylonian mythology.[159] In the same way today's theology has to utilize the present scientific knowledge in order to formulate and proclaim a contemporary doctrine of creation.[160] "The confession of the God of the Christian message as the creator of heaven and earth remains empty, remains a mere confession of the lips, as long as one cannot affirm with good reasons that nature, with which the natural scientist is concerned, has something to do with this God."[161] This also means that the doctrine of creation needs not only to conform to the current natural science but also has to change when there are new scientific descriptions of the world because it always has to reinterpret them.[162]

In order to understand Pannenberg's approach it is necessary to recognize his view of theology as science. He describes theological statements and doctrines as scientific hypotheses and therefore as expressions of temporary

---

[157] Wolfhart Pannenberg, *Contingency and Natural Law*: 74.
[158] Ibid., 74f.
[159] Dürr, Meyer-Abich, Mutschler, Pannenberg, Wuketits, ibid., 107.
[160] Wolfhart Pannenberg, *The Doctrine of Creation and Modern Science*, in: id., *Toward a Theology of Nature: Essays on Science and Faith*, (Louisville, KT: Westminster/John Knox Press, 1993), 45.
[161] Wolfhart Pannenberg, *Contingency and Natural Law*: 74.
[162] Cf. Anja Lebkücher, *Theologie der Natur: Wolfhart Pannenbergs Beitrag zum Dialog zwischen Theologie und Naturwissenschaft*, (Neukirchen-Vluyn: Neukirchener Verlagsgesellschaft, 2011), 152.

knowledge of the truth which has to be proved by experience. Indeed, experience is an important tool in order to define reality, especially in a Methodist theological setting. Empirical knowledge can be a helpful bridge between theology and natural science when it is conscious that it is achieved in different ways. But Pannenberg does not want to admit a difference between theology and natural science because for him they describe one and the same reality. But the critique is justified which insists on the difference between theology as hermeneutical science and natural science. The first one deals more subjectively with interpretations and meanings of a given matter (e.g. of sacred texts) the other one has an objectifying world view and wants to discover universal natural laws. A further difference is also obvious regarding the proofs of insights: Only a scientific hypothesis can be falsified but not a theological statement or doctrine. The latter can only be gradually verified.[163] A dialogue between theology and natural science has to be aware of their common ground of the one reality but also their differences regarding methods and evaluation. In the end they are not alternative but complementary descriptions of the one reality.

It should be noticed that the phrase "dialogue between theology and natural science" also has a disadvantage because it supports the idea of two distinct parties and could solidify the separation. Scientists and Christians are not two mutually exclusive groups at odds with one another but rather there are many Christians who are scientists or work as engineers or technicians. The goal must be that Christians are able to connect their religious and scientific education and to contribute to reconciliation between faith and natural science.[164] On the other hand non-Christian scientists are also human individuals with a particular biographical background and worldview. Their

[163] Cf. Anja Lebkücher, ibid., 49f.56.60.
[164] Anja Lebkücher, ibid., 19.

science deals not only with scientific facts but is also 'personal knowledge'[165] including personal interpretations. Even atheism is not a neutral position as contemporary society sometimes considers. Furthermore everybody has a metaphysical world view which is metaphysically reasoned. There is no reason to doubt that "theology and science are partners in the human quest for truth and understanding, gained through the search for motivated belief. The character of their mutual engagement must reflect this fact."[166]

## Subjects of the Dialogue

In the following I want to discuss three theological subject areas which are linked directly or indirectly to astronomy and could influence crucially the dialogue between theology and natural science: First, the description of the world existing in space and time and the various cosmologies. This is already an important subject in the first biblical creation story when God created space by expanding the firmament (raqia) and made the celestial bodies as 'celestial clocks'. Second is the notion of God's activity in the world and its relation to natural laws defined by science. This subject arises especially from the biblical passages about the movements of celestial bodies according to the reliable ordinances of God. And third, the status of the human beings in the universe and their ethical responsibility for the Earth. Also in view of these topics, Wolfhart Pannenberg was a forward thinker and gave worthwhile ideas.

First, modern astronomy and biblical texts speak differently about the beginning and the end of the world and challenge us to think about cosmology and its theological implications. Initially, we have to notice that 'beginning' and 'end' of the universe are terms describing both time and

---

[165] Cf. John Polkinghorne, *Theology in the Context of Science*: 23ff. referring on Michael Polanyi, who reflects science as to be necessarily an activity of persons.
[166] Ibid., 27.

space. Physics as well as theology deal with these subjects so that they are a meaningful topic for dialogue. "If theology is to function successfully in the context of science, it will need to pay more heed to scientific insight into cosmic timescales."[167] Knowing that the visible universe exists since almost 14 billion years ago and taken this age as a single cosmic 'Year' we would discover that "the time from Abraham to the present day would amount to less than the final ten seconds of the last 'Day'.... The timescales of creation should at least encourage in the theological mind the thought that the creator is not a God in a hurry. It is also highly questionable that the final fulfilment of the present creation is to be expected in the comparatively near future."[168] Additionally, considering the 'world' not only as our home planet Earth but as outer space where the Sun is only a normal star among billions of stars and our Milky Way only a galaxy among billions of galaxies we would frame questions of God's revelation and salvation in a wider context.

Pannenberg is one of the very few German theologians who has reflected on such questions and deliberately confronted theology with insights of natural science. In his theology space and time are relevant topics in the doctrines of God's eternity, the doctrine of creation and the eschatology. He stated: "The idea of God's transcendence also demands space if it is not to be reduced to the logical distinction of the Infinite from everything finite."[169] Biblical metaphors of God's dwelling or appearance show that God is in relation to space and time. Although the space of the universe (geometrical space) and the absolute space of the divine Being (omnipresence of God) must be distinguished[170], "they may go together if we take the first as describing the space of the creaturely world and the second, the immensity of God that constitutes this space.... By his infinity God is present to all things,

---

[167] John Polkinghorne, *Theology in the Context of Science,* 34.
[168] Ibid., 33f.
[169] Wolfhart Pannenberg, *Systematic Theology Vol.2*, Edinburgh: T&T Clark Ltd, 1994), 85.
[170] Cf. Jürgen Moltmann, *God in Creation: A New Theology of Creation and the Spirit of God*, (Minneapolis, MN: Fortress Press, 1993), 156f.

constituting the omnipresence of the space of creation."[171] This description of the distinction and relationship between the space of creation and the space of divine omnipresence is important for the dialogue. It avoids on the one side an incorrect pantheism and on the other hand it persists in the belief of God's activity in space and time.

Time anon is related to space. "There are a number of good reasons – suggested by both philosophical and scientific thought – to consider time and space as inseparable."[172] Pannenberg refers physically to Einstein's relativity theory which connects time, space and energy. Philosophically he claims the priority of time because space is defined by the simultaneity of things that already implies an idea of time. "The concept of time proves to be basic... for it is constitutive for that of space."[173] Pannenberg sees theology and science especially related in the understanding of time. "If space is to be described as the form of simultaneity of phenomena, then the spatialization of time in physics... may be described as an extrapolation of all limited participation in the eternal presence of God, a participation that is granted to us in the experience of our duration in the flow of time."[174] The relation between time and eternity is also an important impulse for the dialogue between theology and science. "Eternity is constitutive for the experience and concept of time. Only if time is basically a unity, i.e., as eternity, can we understand the nexus of that which is separated in its course."[175] Thus the scientific measuring of time implies already a philosophical or theological concept of time and eternity. Additionally, a special contribution of theology to the dialogue with natural science is its understanding of time as the irreversible history of nature (C.F. Weizsäcker: "Nature's appearance of being without history is an

---

[171] Wolfhart Pannenberg, *Systematic Theology* 2: 89.
[172] Wolfhart Pannenberg, *The Doctrine of Creation and Modern Science*: 41.
[173] Wolfhart Pannenberg, *Systematic Theology* 2: 90.
[174] Wolfhart Pannenberg, *The Doctrine of Creation and Modern Science*: 44.
[175] Wolfhart Pannenberg, *Systematic Theology* 2: 92f.

illusion... even the stars are historical."[176]) and the importance of the future as origin for the presence.

Especially the discipline of cosmology deals with the origin, structure and space-time relationship of the universe. Pannenberg is convinced that scientific cosmological theories are highly relevant for theology and looks for consonance between both descriptions of the world. He follows the main stream of scientists (especially referring to C.F. von Weizsäcker)[177] and considers the Big Bang Theory as the currently best reasonable standard model. This cosmological model would also coincide best with the Christian doctrine of *creation ex nihilo*. It offers the possibility to assume theologically (!) a beginning of the universe even if the reconstructions of the history of the still expanding universe "lead only to proximity to this point, not to t = 0, since we cannot determine any physical state for the actual starting point."[178] Pannenberg admits that physics itself "cannot determine the beginning. For this reason we cannot base the thesis that there was a beginning in time directly on the findings or implications of physics."[179] Despite this he holds fast to the belief that "modern cosmology has given an empirical basis...to think of the whole process of the universe as a totality, and if this total process is finite in space and time, then it has to have a temporal beginning" which is not "a beginning 'in' time...but a beginning of time itself."[180] According to Pannenberg, the thought of a beginning of time indicates also its finitude and "the finitude of the world, insofar as its [sic!] has a temporal structure, includes its end."[181] He sees clearly the differences between the biblical eschatology and the end which modern cosmologies describe. There are completely different time frames regarding the remaining time till the end

[176] Carl Friedrich von Weizsäcker, *The History of Nature*, (1948), 8; quoted in: Wolfhart Pannenberg, *Contingency and Natural Law*: 87.
[177] Cf. Wolfhart Pannenberg, *Contingency and Natural Law*: 86ff.
[178] Wolfhart Pannenberg, *Systematic Theology* 2: 155.
[179] Ibid., 156.
[180] Ibid., 157.
[181] Ibid., 157.

as well as completely different expectations what the future will bring (the return of Christ or the so called death by heat or “big crunch”).[182] However, the end of the world and a temporal limited universe would be a perception shared by theology and science. Although Pannenberg sees both, the difficulties of the standard theory regarding the inconceivability of the starting point and the validity conditions of natural laws[183] and the different timeframes and expectations regarding the future, he prefers the standard model to other cosmological models which consider the universe as an infinite, immutable or cyclical process (cf. the Steady State Cosmology of Herrmann Bondi or the Quantum Cosmology of Pascual Jordan).[184] He points out with good reasons "that the multitude of models of a scientific cosmology vying with each other is today by no means conditioned only by differences of the empirical starting points. Ideological interests are at stake."[185] But he could be affected by the same reproach when he emphasizes strongly the consonance between the Christian world view and the Big Bang Theory since both assume "the finiteness and the historical uniqueness of the world process."[186] Even if the Big Bang Theory seems to facilitate currently the dialogue between Christian faith and natural science to a certain extent it is dangerous to base a theology of creation on one special cosmological theory. Future cosmological models could abolish this theory again and theology would be in a defensive situation again as many times before.[187] The dialogue with natural science is a balancing act of taking seriously the scientific results but not binding the doctrine of creation to a certain cosmological theory. It would be more helpful for the dialogue if we stay aware of the differences of subjects and methods in science and theology.

---

[182] Ibid., 157.
[183] Wolfhart Pannenberg, *Contingency and Natural Law*: 89f.
[184] Ibid., 91-96.
[185] Ibid., 95f.
[186] Ibid., 96.
[187] Anja Lebkücher, ibid., 151.

A second important topic of the dialogue between theology and natural science is the question of God's activity in the world and its relation to the natural laws. The description of movements of the various celestial bodies as reliable ordinances of God is a strong biblical impulse for thinking of God as transcendent creator of natural processes who acts also within and through them. This insight avoids a notion of God which sees Him only as acting in the hereafter or in things described throughout history as miraculous. Many of these miraculous events were later seen merely as gaps having been scientifically explained. However, God doesn't intervene in physical processes but enables them and is the ground of every natural order. Pannenberg particularly emphasizes that theology of creation needs to describe the activity of God consistent with natural science – in view of the beginning and the end of the universe as well as every moment of its history.[188] He tries to connect the causality of natural process with the continuous divine action by the notion of God as a force field which is efficacious in every event. The concept of field would be a bridge between theology and natural science. But Pannenberg's idea of God as a field is unfortunately based on some misunderstandings or misinterpretation of physical field concepts and has misleading theological implications, e.g. an understanding of God as a kind of physical field next to others or as an impersonal divine omnipresence.[189] But a metaphorical usage of the term "field" seems to be acceptable in order to signify "the immanent presence of God and the activity of the divine energies in the space and time of creation."[190] This example of a theological implementation of the field concept makes us aware that the dialogue with natural science cannot be only based on analogies and verbal parallels but requires from the theologians a high

[188] Cf. Anja Lebkücher, ibid., 110.
[189] Cf. John Polkinghorne, *Theology in the Context of Science*: 9-11 and Anja Lebkücher, ibid., 66ff. 110ff.
[190] Anja Lebkücher, ibid., 82f.

contextuality by paying attention to the detailed contents and methods of science.[191]

Furthermore the relationship between contingency and natural law has a special importance in Pannenberg's theology of nature which is very relevant for the dialogue. He argues that the world as a whole and every event is not totally determined and defined by natural laws but generally contingent. He defines contingency as "that which is not necessary on the basis of what is past."[192] Already the biblical experience of the reality "is characterized primarily by contingency, particularly contingency of occurrences. New and unforeseen events take place constantly that are experienced as the work of almighty God. Therefore not only this or that individual happening but all occurrences are basically miraculous or wonderful."[193] Pannenberg defines miracles not as breaches of natural laws but as contingent events.[194] This means that contingency doesn't exclude but includes God's action in the natural process.

Otherwise, similarities or connections in occurrences reveal merely in retrospect: "Only by the light that falls backward from the present to the earlier occurrences can we see continuity without negating thereby uniqueness."[195] Already the thinking of the Israelites would include an "eschatological ontology: if only the future will teach what is significant of an event, then the 'essence' of an event or occurrence is never completely finished in the present.... Only in the eschatological future will we be able to look at creation as a whole."[196] This contingency of occurrences is irreconcilable with "a preplanned purposefulness built into the total process" and "a thoroughgoing constancy of forms of natural processes" which "are by definition only abstract partial aspects in the contingent process of

---

[191] Cf. John Polkinghorne, *Theology in the Context of Science,* 11.
[192] Wolfhart Pannenberg, *Contingency and Natural Law*: 116, footnote 11.
[193] Ibid., 76.
[194] Cf. Anja Lebkücher, ibid., 129.
[195] Wolfhart Pannenberg, *Contingency and Natural Law*: 84.
[196] Ibid, 83.

occurrences."[197] This leads Pannenberg to the insight that the appearance of laws of nature is itself contingent. "The existence of certain laws and of regular order as such can be considered ... as a contingent fact."[198] Even if a law of nature is characterized essentially by its repeatability, the world process as a whole is, according to the second law of thermodynamics, irreversible and unrepeatable.[199] "If the world process as a whole represents a unique process that as a whole is unrepeatable, then it also cannot be understood in its entirely as the application of a law."[200] Whereas the Greek conception of the cosmos and later classical physics was widely determined by the faith in an eternal and unchangeable order of the universe, the Old Testament already conceived these orders "dependent on the contingency of the divine will, not only in view of their origin but also in view of their continuance."[201] Pannenberg states that this view on the regularities of nature would also permit exceptions and changes of natural laws. Contemporary physics, especially quantum physics would reveal "that determinism is an illusion".[202] In the end Pannenberg's emphasis on contingency is an attempt to connect natural science and belief in creation. "When natural science, in seeking laws and especially the origin of the present world with its forms and laws, comes upon contingent conditions and events, it opens nature up in such a way that the Christian can discover the expression of the creative act of God."[203] Contingency and the belief in creation are dependent on each other. The contingency of occurrences is fundamental for the understanding of nature as creation. "Contingency in the sense of something that is not given as necessary by what already exists is an indispensable element of creative producing" and has "in view of that which is to be produced ...

[197] Ibid., 84.
[198] Ibid., 98.
[199] Ibid., 88.
[200] Ibid., 106.
[201] Ibid., 76.
[202] Ibid., 77.
[203] Ibid., 98.

essentially the character of creating love."[204] That this contingency also enables the continuity of natural laws and other forms of uniformity in natural occurrences is an expression of God's faithfulness.[205]

A third important topic of the dialogue between theology and natural science is the status of human beings in the universe and their ethical responsibility for creation. In a cosmic perspective human beings are only "inhabitants of a mere speck of cosmic dust"[206] and a time-limited species among others in the evolutionary process. On the other hand the existence and development of human life in the universe itself seems to be very unique and has required very special physical conditions, e.g. regarding the size of our universe. "In fact a universe that was much smaller than ours would not have lasted long enough to have been able to evolve carbon-based life of our kind of complexity. In a real sense, all that vast multitude of stars is necessary for the possibility of our being here as the inhabitants of Earth."[207] Additionally, the origin and development of life is based on other natural constants, like the close balance between the expansion of the universe and the cohesive effect of gravity within or the age of the universe and the sufficient availability of hydrogen by those nuclear furnaces in the stars so that other chemical elements could emerge. Not least, other astronomical conditions, like the distance from the Sun to the Earth, the effects of the Moon on the Earth's orbit, the inclination of the axis of the Earth and the composition of its atmosphere etc. are also very important for the existence of life. It seems that only little variations of the precise natural constants would have obstructed the development of complex, intelligent life. "In other words, a universe capable of evolving carbon-based life is a very particular universe indeed,

[204] Ibid., 98.
[205] Ibid., 109.
[206] John Polkinghorne, *Theology in the Context of Science*: 35.
[207] Ibid., 35.

'finely tuned' in the character of its basic physical process."[208] These surprising facts have led to the so called "anthropic principle" which is an often discussed argument in the dialogue between theology and natural science.[209] There are different versions of the anthropic principle. The so called 'weak anthropic principle' states only "that our presence in the universe implies that its nature must be consistent with its having evolved carbon-based life...The laws and circumstances of the universe must be compatible with our presence in it as observer."[210] It doesn't explain this fact but notes only tautologically: We are here because we are here. The stronger version of the anthropic principle claims that the goal of the fine-tuned universe is the origin of human life. It "alleges that the universe must be capable of evolving life".[211] This teleological perspective goes beyond a scientific explanation and can be connected to a metaphysical explanation or a belief in a creator. The strongest version of the anthropic principle asserts additionally that human, intelligent life is constitutive of the universe and cannot disappear as long as the universe exists.[212]

Pannenberg also refers to the anthropic principle in its stronger version but he is aware that this is neither a scientific argument for the existence of God nor for the necessity of the existence of human life. The anthropic principle "cannot claim much value as a physical explanation, but it shows very impressively that de facto the universe is so oriented as to provide conditions for the emergence of intelligent beings."[213] It is certainly not a cosmological proof of an intelligent author but shows that "the emergence of life and humans cannot be adjudged to be a matter of chance that might well not have happened."[214] The physical thesis that the normative natural constants

---

[208] John Polkinghorne, *Science and Theology*: 36.
[209] Cf. Anja Lebkücher, ibid., 156.
[210] John Polkinghorne, *Science and Theology:* 36, 73.
[211] Ibid., 37.
[212] Anja Lebkücher, ibid., 156.
[213] Wolfhart Pannenberg, *Systematic Theology* 2: 115.
[214] Ibid., 127.

have enabled life does not necessitate the insight "that the world was created for our sake or in orientation to us."[215] Only the belief in God which recognizes the whole universe as its creation can answer the questions *why* life has appeared, what the meaning of life is and what its goal will be. Still more, "theological interpretation may go further and say that we see here the economy of the divine work of creation relative to the incarnation of the divine Logos in a man."[216] For Pannenberg the goal of the universe is not the emergence of human beings but the incarnation of the Logos. "Only in the event of incarnation comes the working of the Logos throughout creation to fulfilment."[217] All these insights show us that the anthropic principle can be a fruitful meeting point for the dialogue between theology and science but it doesn't necessarily include a theological interpretation of the presence of God or the meaning of life.

Based on the particular status of human beings in the universe is our ethical responsibility for the planet Earth. Theologically this special responsibility is reasoned in biblical anthropology which considers human beings as *imago dei* (Gn 1:27; Ps 8 etc.). The claim that human beings are God's image on Earth means that they "rule over other earthly creatures as God's *representatives* and in his name; they are God's *counterpart* on earth, the counterparts to whom he wants to talk, and who is intended to respond to him; and they are the appearance of God's splendour, and his glory on earth."[218] Especially the first aspect connected to the doctrine of the *dominium terrae* could be a positive argument in the dialogue between theology and science which affirms the scientific and technological progress. On the other hand we need to be aware that the specific designation to rule follows from the dignity of being *imago dei* and not vice versa![219] A

---

[215] Ibid., 133.
[216] Ibid., 115.
[217] Ibid., 114.
[218] Jürgen Moltmann, ibid., 220f.
[219] Moltmann, ibid., 220f.224f.

consequence of a misinterpreted doctrine of the *dominium terrae* is the misuse of science and technology which leads to the oppression of other creatures (and consequently other people too!) and the destruction of the conditions of life on our planet. Therefore an important part of the dialogue between theology and natural science is the search for the ethical criteria for natural science itself as well as for its technical implementation and consequences. The ethical arguments cannot be contributed by natural science itself because of its objects and methods but results essentially from philosophical and theological reflections. In concrete terms, in a dialogue with astronomy Christians are able to address an ethic of the "care for the environment in a cosmic setting".[220] Thereby they can use an approach based on the biblical doctrine of creation and the idea of *imago dei* in order to emphasize the importance of the creation and of our stewardship. Furthermore, Christian ethics needs to pay attention also to its eschatological foundation. This eschatological perspective strengthens even more the care for the environment by the "emphasis not only on God's purposes in creation but also in new creation."[221] Continuity and discontinuity between creation and new creation need to be held together in a description of Christian ethics. Beyond ethical questions which are linked to life on Earth there are such questions which address the life of extraterrestrial beings and the encounter with them or human life beyond the atmosphere of the Earth. Whereas the existence of aliens and the ensuing theological and ethical consequences are interesting but currently irrelevant, the latter possibility seems to be becoming more real in the coming decades and indeed has an ethical relevance. The building of cities on the Moon or the near planets (e.g. Mars) as well as the so-called "terraforming" are already discussed and in the process of planning.[222] Next to the hope to find extraterrestrial resources for humankind

---

[220] David Wilkinson, ibid., 180ff.
[221] Ibid., 180.
[222] Ibid., 180f.

these plans also include dangerous ideas of escaping (only for the rich and powerful!) from the overpopulated, exploited and polluted planet Earth. But these imaginations are neither a way out of the ecological crisis nor suspend us from our responsibility for our home planet. It shows us that we have to take more seriously the universal and eschatological horizon of Christian theology and ethics and to bring it into the dialogue. "With the perspective of the whole Universe we are forced to see the action of God in both continuity and discontinuity [between] creation [and] new creation. The maintaining of the Earth's environment, its biodiversity and natural resources is not just for present or future generations but part of co-operating with God in the process of transformation."[223]

## Methodist Impulses

There are some impulses from the heritage of Methodism which could be helpful for the dialogue with natural science. First, it is interesting that John Wesley himself could be seen as a pioneer of the dialogue with the natural science of his day.[224] The emerging Enlightenment and the Industrial Revolution in England challenged him and the Methodist movement, provoking theological reflection and social action. Wesley was himself very well-educated not only in (church) history, classical languages but also in physics and medicine. "His favourite scientific topics were astronomy, electricity, earthquakes physiology, and volcanoes."[225] He was familiar with the writings of members of Britain's Royal Society which was the oldest and most famous learned society for science. However, Wesley didn't only

---

[223] Ibid., 181 referring to J.J.Davis, *Will There be New Work in the New Creation? Evangelical Review of Theology 31 (3)*, 256-273.

[224] A bibliography regarding the new historical studies about John Wesley's relationship with natural science is available on the website of 'Wesley Nexus': http://www.wesnex.org/H_AboutUs_History_WesleyScience.html last access: 1 November 2011

[225] J.W. Haas, Jr., *John Wesley's Vision of Science in the Service of Christ*; quotation from the website: http://www.asa3.org/ASA/PSCF/1995/PSCF12-95Haas.html last access: 1 November 2011

accumulate knowledge of natural science but also published books and articles on scientific subjects, like the folk medicine handbook *Primitive Physic* (1747), the multipart edition of *A Survey of the Wisdom of God in Creation, or, A Compendium of Natural Philosophy* (1763), or the *Desideratum, or, Electricity Made Plain and Useful* (1760). Not the least important are his published sermons "which reflect an active and appreciative interest in the natural world and scientific progress."[226] These publications served especially to educate common people as well as his itinerant preachers. The fact that John Wesley was very interested in natural science and that his adherents "moved to the cultural centre through an unquenchable passion for education"[227] is a special motivation for Methodists today to also be engaged in the dialogue with science and involved in education, especially among people of the underclass. The latter makes us also aware of the social dimension of the dialogue. If knowledge is power then the question arises who has free access to knowledge, education and science. Today we are experiencing again that the education of people is more and more a question of class and income. Additionally, in a globalized world the power of education plays an important role for cultural transfer and 'globalization via soft power'.[228] Thus the dialogue between natural science and religion is not only about the theoretical question of God and defining reality in general but includes necessarily a social-ethical component. The Methodist approach to the dialogue between religion and science make us aware of the question of who has the power to define social reality and address the ethical and social responsibility of science and research.

---

[226] Ibid., quotation from the website: http://www.asa3.org/ASA/PSCF/1995/PSCF12-95Haas.html last access: 1 November 2011

[227] David, Hempton, *Methodism-Empire of the Spirit*, (New Haven and London:Yale University Press, 2005), 31.

[228]Cf. Joerg Rieger, *Globalization and Theology*, (Nashville, TN: Abigdon Press, 2010), 37f.

Next to the social contextuality of Wesley's interest in natural science we can also learn from his manner how to reflect theologically new scientific insights. His reflection is based on the 'quadrilateral' which connects Scripture (which has priority), experience, reason and tradition in order to define and interpret reality. Initially, we observe a constructive openness to new scientific insights without fear of contact because Wesley could honour reason as a gift of God which helped appropriately to understand and describe the world. "He maintained an active interest in the development of the new science valuing it for the benefits it brought to human happiness."[229] Otherwise he also knew that reason and science are limited and need to be balanced out with the other parts of the quadrilateral like Scripture and tradition. "He encouraged his preachers and broader constituency to gain an understanding of the new science from a world view which saw God as creator and sustainer, ... was alert to the problems [of] natural theology... [and] pursued a middle road which considered both faith and reason."[230] Even if Wesley's approach to natural science could be sometime criticized as too selective, intentionally and theologically conservative "he mixed rationalistic orthodoxy and pietistic theology with natural philosophy in ways that allowed his followers to appreciate and participate in the study of God's creation."[231] Furthermore, the Wesleyan quadrilateral with its emphasis on the central importance of the Scripture could encourage theology to enter the dialogue with an explicitly biblical approach which would introduce a more narrative thinking instead of the prevailing philosophical approach and its rationalistic base.[232]

---

[229] J.W. Haas, Jr., ibid., quotation from the website: http://www.asa3.org/ASA/PSCF/1995/PSCF12-95Haas.html
last access: 01.11.2011
[230] Ibid., quotation from the website: http://www.asa3.org/ASA/PSCF/1995/PSCF12-95Haas.html
last access: 01.11.2011
[231] Ibid., quotation from the website: http://www.asa3.org/ASA/PSCF/1995/PSCF12-95Haas.html
last access: 01.11.2011
[232] Cf. David Wilkinson, ibid., 55f

In the end Methodism helps us to understand the dialogue between theology and science as a special kind of mission which is a part of the *mission dei* in our universe. Wesley's diverse engagement in the dialogue with science, be it on the intellectual level of the philosophical-theological discourse (including his apologetical efforts), or in a practical way by education or medical care, could be interpreted as missional ministry - not only *for* others but *with* others. This ministry brings together different people so that the dialogue between theology and science becomes an encounter *between people* of different world views and professions. Such ministry raises the question of God and the meaning of life in many ways and includes the proclamation and implementation of the Gospel. Such ministry gives people orientation and hope in a complex reality and trains them in loving stewardship of the natural world. The goal is to 'spread scriptural holiness throughout the land' which comprises personal and social life (including science) as well as the sanctification of the whole universe as God's beloved creation.

# CHAPTER SIX:
# THE ASTRONOMICAL OBSERVATORY PROJECT

## The History of the Astronomical Observatory[233]

The construction of the astronomical observatory in Dresden-Gönnsdorf started already in 1972/73 and was inaugurated on 2 July 1976 by the Dresden University of Technology. The location of the observatory, called Gönnsdorfer Höhe (Gönnsdorf Heights), was a preferred astronomical observation point. The university conducted research in its observatory with a 12" astrographic camera which regularly took pictures of the night sky in order to register and to measure celestial bodies. As the light pollution was increasing by the nearby city and the footage for the astrograph became scarcely available the university stopped the scientific research at this place in 1996 and built a new observatory on another location. There was an agreement between the municipal council and the university that the old observatory should become a non-profit, public observatory as soon as the new observatory of the university would be finished. But meanwhile the ownership of the old observatory had changed by the incorporation of the region into the city of Dresden in 1999. The new property management was not under contract to the former agreement so that the old observatory was vacant and decayed more and more. In 2006 the university took out all astronomical instruments and distributed them among anyone interested. But the former mayor and today's municipal administrator of the region, Hans-Jürgen Behr, and a municipal councillor, Renate Franz, strove for the repurchase and reconstruction of the old observatory and its non-profit use – for some years without success. Finally, in 2009, the Verein zur Förderung der Jugend e.V. (Registered Association for the Advancement of Youth,

[233] Hans-Jürgen Eichhorn, *Sternwarte- Dresden-Gönnsdorf - Chronik*, (self-published, undated); partly available on the website: http://www.sternwarte-goennsdorf.de/vorgeschichte.php last access: 13 December 2011

founded in 1998) could purchase the old astronomical observatory, financially supported by the municipal council, in order to enable its public use.

At the time of takeover the astronomical observatory was in bad shape: its inventory was completely removed, all utilities like electricity, water supply and telecommunication were broken, the dome lacked motors and was therefore not movable, the building was covered with graffiti and the surrounding grounds were unkempt. Only the building itself was structurally sound. It was obvious that strenuous efforts would be necessary in order to restore and operate the astronomical observatory again. Otherwise, the still existing building of the observatory and its previous history was a good starting point for initiating dialogue with natural science in the context of Astronomy. Also in this case previous history has provided space for a new story. Additionally, the great openness among people who lived near the observatory and were interested in its further operation nourished the expectations of its rebuilding and reopening.

### The Foundation and the Progress of the Project

As already mentioned the **Verein zur Förderung der Jugend e.V.**[234] became the new owner of the astronomical observatory. This registered association is a non profit organisation which does not have an explicit ideological or denominational background. Its purpose is to mainly provide low-threshold, socio-pedagogical activities and personal supporting measures for children and youth between 6 and 27 years in order to strengthen their individual development and self-discovery process as well as their social competence. This association is operating various projects like a children and youth club, a school garden, a fanfare ensemble and is also the legal provider of the

234 The following facts and more information about the Verein zur Förderung der Jugend e.V. are available on the internet: http://www.kjhpep.de/index.php?start
last access: 16 December 2011;
http://www.stadtjugendring-dresden.de/index.php?id=14,36,0,0,1,0
last access: 16 December 2011

astronomical observatory. The latter was purchased with the objective to enable a meaningful leisure activity for children and youth, to give the surrounding schools the possibility of astronomical observations and to invite hobby astronomers and other interested citizens to use this facility for practical astronomy and related scientific subjects.[235] But the association had no staff to restore and operate the astronomical observatory. It was necessary to find volunteers, who would promote, organize and accomplish the work. At this point there emerged a great chance for collaboration between the association and people who would be interested in this project.

Indeed, in April 2009 the *Interessengemeinschaft Sternwarte Dresden-Gönnsdorf* (Interest Group of the Observatory Dresden-Gönnsdorf) was founded. Interestingly, the founding of the interest group in 2009 coincided with the **"International Year of Astronomy"**, proclaimed by the UNESCO.[236] It had the exciting slogan: "The Universe – Yours to Discover". The occasion was the 400th anniversary of the first use of an astronomical telescope by Galileo Galilei and the publication of Johannes Kepler's groundbreaking book *Astronomia Nova* which described the physical laws regarding the movements of the celestial bodies. The International Year of Astronomy emphasized the great importance of astronomy for all cultures and was a platform which informed people worldwide about astronomical basic knowledge, the newest discoveries of astronomy and the necessity of (astronomical) education in order to contribute to a more just and peaceful society. At the same time it was a great chance for communication between scientists and hobby astronomers as well as between various astronomical projects.[237] The public interest in astronomy was aroused enormously by this

---

[235] Hans-Jürgen Eichhorn, ibid. , partly available on the website: http://www.sternwarte-goennsdorf.de/vorgeschichte.php
last access: 13 December 2011

[236] Comprehensive information about the International Year of Astronomy are available on the official website: http://www.astronomy2009.org
last access: 17 December 2011

[237] See the vision of the IYA2009: http://www.astronomy2009.org/general/

event and gave much hope for support and sponsoring of our observatory project which was depicted at the International Year of Astronomy website too.[238] These facts show that next to the historical links and the societal context the attention of the media are important for the founding of a project and its publicity.

The **founding of the interest group** was on 29 April 2009. Already in March there were articles in the newspapers *Hochlandkurier* and *Sächsische Zeitung* which reported about the future plans regarding the astronomical observatory and called for interested people who would found an interest group in order to renovate and operate the observatory. The municipal councillor, Renate Franz, was stated in that article as contact person who would arrange the location and the date of the foundation meeting.

Thirteen people - eight men and five women – were attracted by the newspaper article and came together on the mentioned day at a restaurant near the astronomical observatory in order to establish the interest group. All of them were hobby astronomers with diverse professions like teacher, physician, politician, engineer, littérateur, patent attorney, entrepreneur, craftsman and pastor. The age of the founding members was between 40 and 70 years. Meanwhile the interest group grew up to eighteen members including two youths. All people are Germans – one person with Japanese roots that enriches the cultural background of the group. There is also a diversity of ideological beliefs: About 45 percent are Christians (e.g. Methodists and Lutherans) and 55 percent would consider themselves as atheists.

The **founding meeting** started with the self-introduction of the people, talking about their linkage to the hobby of astronomy and expressing the dreams and expectations regarding the future of the observatory project. During the

---

last access: 17 December 2011

[238] http://www.astronomy2009.org/news/updates/682/
last access: 29 January 2012

meeting the vision became clear: restoration of the old astronomical observatory if possible till the end of the year 2009 and after that operating it as a facility for astronomical observation and education as well as a meeting point for all interested people who want to communicate about astronomy and related subjects. The goal of the founding meeting was the establishing of an interest group that plans and implements the reconstruction and operation of the observatory. The legal status of the newly founded interest group became clarified and defined as an associated interest group institutionally connected to the *Verein zur Förderung der Jugend e.V.* but working and funding itself autonomously. Two people are members of the registered association as well as the interest group so that the intercommunication would be guaranteed. The advantage of this associated status of the interest group was obvious because the *Verein zur Förderung der Jugend e.V.* would fulfil all legal requirements (e.g. attestation of the non-profit status, insurance) and administrative necessities (e.g. to issue donation receipts) whereas the interest group could focus on its project work without having to deal with complex German bureaucracy. In a way a disadvantage of this associated status was that the *Verein zur Förderung der Jugend e.V.* considers itself as ideologically neutral so that an explicit Christian agenda couldn't be fixed in the statutes of the interest group. For instance, the Rules of Operation mention only a dialogue between natural science and philosophy but not theology.[239] However, in practice were there no obstacles to addressing Christian topics and performing a dialogue with theology. So in summary this very well functioning collaboration can be an example how Christians and non-Christians work together in secular associations and generate synergies for a common purpose.

The founding meeting also had to deal with the **question of leadership and personnel**. The group appointed the municipal councillor, Renate Franz, as

[239] See the appendix: Rules of Operation – Attachment 6

leader and secretary of the interest group and staffed the treasurer, the chronicler, and homepage administrator. All group members would work as volunteers. Additionally, the personal data, the professions and the capabilities of all group members were registered in order to involve everybody's capabilities in the further work. The group recognized the task for the near future to develop a manual which would establish the goals of the observatory project and its implementation as well as regulate questions of leadership and personnel. This task needed some time for experimentation and experiences till in 2011 the already mentioned Rules of Operation were completed and regulated sufficiently all issues of personnel (vocation, task fields, tenures, elections, substitutes) on a democratic basis.

The biggest challenge for the next months was the **planning, funding and implementation of the restoration** of the observatory. Many following meetings, from the founding of the interest group to the complete restoration in October 2009, dealt with building operations.[240] Members of the interest group and other volunteers spent many hours and days working. Local companies and craftsmen supported the renovation with expertise, material and work, mostly without payment. The following building and restoration activities were accomplished: cleaning up and preparation of the surrounding grounds (May 2009), installation of the electrical wiring, the breaker box and the lightening protection (June 2009), scaffolding the observatory (July 2009) and repainting of the dome outside (August-September 2009), graffiti removal (October 2009) and spray on the logo of the International Year of the Astronomy with its slogan on the external facade (November 2009), scaffolding and cleaning up of the dome inside and restoration of the dome's mechanism (November 2009), painting of the observation hall (December 2009) as well as of the dome inside (July 2010), production and installation of

[240] Hans-Jürgen Eichhorn, ibid., partly available on the website: http://www.sternwarte-goennsdorf.de/vorgeschichte.php
last access: 13 December 2011

the monumental telescope column (April 2010), floor covering at the observation hall and tiling of the ground-floor (October 2010), fitting of the dome with computer-controllable electric motors and finally the installation of a computerized 14" Meade Mirror Telescope (October 2010).

To summarize, all these reconstruction activities strengthened the cohesion and identity of the interest group which gathered people of different ages, professions, worldviews and denominations. Additionally, they aroused the attention and solidarity of people nearby who were interested in astronomy or in the preservation of the observatory which was shining now in a new splendour. Every restored and finished part of the observatory became an artifact which told the story of shared interests, common efforts, arduous sacrifices and cheering success. From time to time the group celebrated "short-term wins"[241] and held festive meetings which expressed thankfulness for the achieved progress, rewarded the people involved, helped to stay focused on the common goals, proclaimed the further steps and invited new supporters.

A great highlight was the **inauguration of the renovated astronomical observatory** on 28 October 2010. About 80 guests from politics, economy, sciences and society came to its re-opening and stood in front of the observatory. Punctually at 6 pm the dome of the observatory was opened and out of the illuminated observatory sounded the "Ode an die Freude" (Ode to Joy). After the welcoming of the guests by the leader of the interest group I addressed the audience with an inauguration speech[242] which was about a pastor's connection to astronomy and the observatory project, the differentiated relation between science and theology and the dedication of the observatory as a place of learning, wonder, philosophizing and tolerant dialogue between people with different worldviews and beliefs. I ended the speech with the reading of Psalm 8 and a blessing for the people who

[241] Cf. John P. Kotter, *Leading Change,* (Bosten, MA: Havard Business School Press, 1996), 117ff.
[242] See the appendix: Inauguration Speech

attended the inauguration and prayed for those who would visit the observatory in the future. After the opening ceremony which included the cutting of a cord in front of the entrance of the observatory a welcome party took place at a recreation centre nearby. There was a festive catering, a cultural program provided by pupils and a presentation about the reconstruction of the observatory and its future possibilities. A highlight was the delivery of an old wooden tablet which commemorated the first construction period (1973-1976) when the observatory was built by the Dresden University of Technology. Professors of the university had saved it from destruction and brought it as a gift. The inauguration celebration ended with an observation of Jupiter and its moons by the new mirror telescope.
The place where the dialogue between faith and natural science could take place was now created and dedicated. The inauguration of the observatory also showed the importance of common celebration and rites. The observatory became a place where people could experience that science and vision, histories and stories, knowledge and belief, reason and emotion belong together.

## Public Relations and Sponsoring

From the beginning the interest group was aware that the project would need a lot of public support and solidarity. Thus it has paid special attention to public relations in different areas. A first step was to think about the presence and the image of the group in the public. Already after the first meetings the group decided to symbolize its corporate identity by developing a **logo** of the observatory project.[243] This logo has become visible on all publications and advertising materials like flyers, bumper stickers and t-shirts.

---

[243] See the appendix: Logo

Another important tool to reach the public was the creation of a **website**[244] which offers information about the history of the observatory, the progress of its reconstruction, and about the observation program and sponsoring. The website also provides material for astronomical lessons (on the intranet), the possibility of making contact with the interest group and an electronic application procedure for interested people or groups who want to visit the observatory. Important for the dialogue is the linkage between the websites of the observatory and of the Emmaus UMC.

The interest group has always maintained contact with the **media.** The local press has been regularly informed, e.g. about the plans of the interest group, the progress of the restoration of the observatory, special funding activities in the public, the honouring of special sponsors, and after the inauguration, about the astronomical observation program. In one case even the local television station (MDR) reported about the observatory during the partial solar eclipse on 4 January 2011.

Furthermore the interest group was present at diverse **community and churchly events** with an information desk, transportable astronomical telescopes and a kiosk. Group members introduced and promoted the observatory project at diverse city festivals (Elbhangfest, Hochlandfest), at a local school festival (Schulfest in Leuben), a hiking day for families (Familienwandertag), sports meeting (Weißiger Sportfest), and at a promotional event at a restaurant (course of lectures at the Gasthaus zum Hochland). The contact to the whole membership of the Emmaus UMC was supported by the disclosure of information about the observatory at church services, congregation council meetings and churchly events, e.g. children's festivals. Additionally, the interest group has made contact to other astronomical observatories (e.g. Sternwarte Radebeul), meeting points of hobby astronomers (Teleskoptreffen in Jeßnik), the astronomical faculty of

[244] www.sternwarte-goennsdorf.de
last access: 29 January 2012

the Dresden University of Technology and a research institute (Helmholtz-Centre) in Dresden-Rossendorf. The latter connections helped not only to get the advice of experts but also to find competent dialogue partners outside the interest group.

An important task of the interest group has been **fundraising and sponsoring.** The International Year of Astronomy aroused great interest in astronomical projects among many people including potential sponsors. This occasion boosted the expectation of getting public funds in order to finance the restoration of the observatory and the astronomical instruments but this hope was soon dashed. So the group had to find other creative ways of fundraising. First, the members of the interest group set a good example and donated money (e.g by monthly contributions) and continued to work for free. A further creative idea was the creation of a big puzzle of the astronomical observatory whose pieces were disclosed for a donation of 10 Euros each with the sponsors' names being published on the website.[245] Further sources of income were the public presentations of the observatory in the form of astronomical lessons (e.g. at a restaurant and the university), open house at the observatory which included auctions and promotional merchandising. But the biggest contributions of funding the project came from local companies and craftsmen who took notice of the observatory project in the media or were contacted by funding letters[246] or by phone. Often they donated the material for the reconstruction of the observatory and worked for free. The same holds true for the acquisition of the astronomical instruments: A municipal savings bank sponsored a transportable sun telescope, a local drainage and waste water company a 10" mirror telescope and an American telescope manufacturer four telescopes of different sizes. The latter company also loaned the big 14" mirror telescope which is now the main telescope at

[245] http://www.sternwarte-goennsdorf.de/puzzle.php
last access: 22 December 2011
[246] See the appendix: Funding Letters

the astronomical observatory till we can buy our own 16" mirror telescope. Other equipment like oculars, computers and astronomical wall charts were sponsored too. All benefactors who have contributed to the restoration and operation of the observatory became honoured on a display at the observatory and on its website.[247] Also Emmaus UMC, single members and entrepreneurs among them, has supported the project by donations, commodity contributions and volunteer work.

To summarize: The project has become an example for successful team work and collaboration between people and nonprofit organizations[248] with different worldviews, capabilities and interests. It has especially proven that Christians and non-Christians can work together for a common goal when they accept, respect and support each other. The fact that Christians serve society, not separate from secular organisations or in competition with them, but with and within them is a great insight for the future mission of the church in East Germany.

---

[247] http://www.sternwarte-goennsdorf.de/sponsoren.php
last access: 29 January 2011

[248] Cf. also Leslie R. Crutchfield, Heather McLeod Grant, *Forces for Good: The Six Practices of High-Impact Nonprofits,* (San Franzisco, CA: Jossey-Bass, 2008), especially about *"Nurture nonprofit networks"*, p.22, 105ff.

# CHAPTER SEVEN:
# THE PRACTICE OF THE DIALOGUE

## The Model of the Practical Dialogue

Astronomy is one of the oldest and most popular sciences and therefore very useful in order to initiate a public dialogue between Christian faith and natural science. Regarding the audience, this dialogue can include an inner reflection of a single person who is a believer and an intellectual, a discourse among Christians who want to ponder the relationship between faith and natural science, or a dialogue between Christians and non-Christians who want to discuss together this topic. The following model is theologically based on a Trinitarian understanding of the dialogue and also confirmed by the practice of discourse in the context of the observatory project. It can be summarized by four terms: INTERCONNECTION, INFORMATION, INTERCHANGE and INTERACTION.

**First, INTERCONNECTION** means to bring Christians and people of other beliefs and worldviews together in order to provide a fruitful discourse and intellectual exchange of ideas. Creating a meeting point of diverse people and various ideas is always a great chance for new contacts, interesting dialogue, and new insights among the participants. When the present group is very homogeneous, interconnection can also mean that only one person informs and inspires people with other perspectives or worldviews in order to challenge and widen their horizons.

**Second, INFORMATION** includes the communication of the necessary astronomical knowledge in order to get a competent understanding of the scientific topics. People learn more about the scientific facts and exchange their expertise. The extension of philosophical, theological and ethical knowledge among the dialogue partners is also necessary in order to create a dialogue on an equal footing. All dialogue partners need a certain level of basic knowledge of the fields involved as the basis of competent debates.

Common learning and mutual teaching is an important purpose of the observatory project.

**Third, INTERCHANGE** stands here for the step beyond the only scientific perspective on the one hand and beyond the only religious worldview on the other hand in order to exchange views and arguments of people with different beliefs and generate a fair dialogue. The intention is to better see the complexity of the world and getting a more complementary view on reality. Christians become more competent to connect their faith with scientific insights in order to formulate a contemporary creed. Secular intellectuals get interested in Christian faith and discover its potential and meaning for personal, professional and social life.

**Fourth, INTERACTION** means a call to practical collaboration and common action of the different dialogue partners. This can be an agreement for further dialogue on other topics but also concrete collaboration for the public good. The observatory project itself provides a variety of opportunities for common practical work in areas of construction work, administration, public relations, popular scientific research and education. Christians and non-Christians work together and contribute to the welfare of society, e.g. by offering astronomy lessons at the observatory as well was at schools and other facilities. Such common action unites different people, supports mutual understanding and implements the mission *with* others.

The following sections will describe the practical implementation of this model in the areas of astronomical observation, lectures about astronomy and taking and analyzing a survey.

## Astronomical Observations

INTERCONNECTION:

The observatory project enables and supports the dialogue in various ways, first of all by astronomical observations. Since the completed restoration and inauguration in October 2010 the astronomical observatory has attracted many people of different ages, professions, classes and worldviews who are interested in astronomy. Hobby astronomers of all types were among them as well as teachers of various fields, scientists from the University of Technology or other research institutes and also staff of neighbouring astronomical observatories. Mostly groups visited the astronomical observatory, e.g. kindergartners, pupils of basic and high schools (gymnasiums), and churchly youth, senior and clergy groups. Generally, there are two ways of creating a meeting at the astronomical observatory: first, the astronomical observatory opens the door for the public at fixed times (announced in the media) and provides observations of different celestial bodies or extraordinary astronomical events. In this case the group of observers is very diverse, people come and go and the dialogue takes place often in a way of one-on-one conversation. The second opportunity of visiting the astronomical observatory is the application of a group on the observatory website which enables a more specific guided tour, teaching and discourse appropriate to the audience. In this case the dialogue can be more focused on a particular topic and the reflection goes deeper. Next to these two opportunities contacts with interested people are also possible when the interest group performs events with astronomical instruments and telescopes outside the observatory, e.g. at schools or city festivals.

INFORMATION:

Whenever people are gathered at the astronomical observatory they are welcomed by members of the interest group and get an introduction of its history, the actual state of the project and the function of the observatory and its telescopes. According to the visitor's level of knowledge there is a short lesson about the basics of astronomy (e.g. structure and movements of the celestial bodies or the use of a star map) and special information about the objects and the process of the observation. Currently the observatory conducts astronomical observations with a computerized 14" mirror telescope which can provide impressive images of the Moon, planets, stars, star clusters and nebulas. The lunar craters, Jupiter and its moons, Venus with its crescent phases and the Orion Nebula are favour objects for observation. Additionally, there are some smaller mirror telescopes which can be operated outside the observatory by the visitors themselves. A special astronomical instrument is the transportable sun telescope with an integrated H-alpha filter that allows direct observations of our home star with its solar spots and prominences. Such observations of the Sun and its eclipses are often very impressive for the audiences. When the partial solar eclipse on 4 January 2011 was visible and the sun rose as a crescent, the local media reported this observation at the observatory which was especially arranged for school classes.

INTERCHANGE:

Empirically, astronomical observations easily open the opportunity to go beyond scientific matters and raise many questions, e.g. of the immensity and purpose of the universe, the existence and action of a Creator God, the fine tuned conditions and the wonder of life on Earth, the meaning and destiny of human life - or most philosophically: Why is there something rather than nothing? The participation in an astronomical observation on a starry night and the knowledge of astronomical data like the incredible extent of space and time in the universe, the number and distances of stars, the sizes and structure of galaxies etc. produces mostly an existential experience which leads people of different worldviews to the limits of their imagination and awakes spontaneous amazement. Like Immanuel Kant said: Two things fill my mind with ever new increasing wonder and awe, the more often I reflect upon them: the starry heaven above me and the moral law within me.[249] Greek philosophy asserted that amazement is the source of human thinking.

---

[249] Epitaph of Immanuel Kant, Königsberg, quoted in: Owen Gingerich, *God's Universe,* (Cambridge, MA: Havard University Press, 2006), 81.

Plato considered the view of the firmament, the stars and the sun as the origin of the human desire for the examination of nature and as the beginning of philosophy. In the same way Aristotle described amazement as the crucial impulse for philosophical thinking. Later, many philosophers, theologians and scientists of all types (even atheists) experienced the moment of amazement while observing the starry sky, and sometimes had a mystical experience.[250] The amazed observer obviously leaves the level of scientific objectivity and comes into an inner relationship with the observed matters which are not passive objects any longer but act upon the observer.[251] Scientific observation can shift into an inner experience of unity as has been described as Oneness with the Universe (as the totality of reality) or with God. Christian theology can help to identify such mystical experience as "encounter with God in the mode of immanence"[252] and refer to a "mystical spirituality of the open eyes"[253] which connects the scientific and spiritual perception of the world.

Various astronomical observations and talks with Christian and non-Christian people and groups have confirmed that amazement and wonder can be a link between natural science and human disciplines as well as between science and religion. The wondering reaction of the observers has proved that amazement is a meeting point where reason and faith meet, sometimes including a moment of awe.[254] It helps people with a strong rationalistic way of thinking or even atheistic ideology to ask theological questions and overcome a strict materialistic worldview. But it also reminds religious people that faith and science are not contradictions but require each other and need to be

---

[250] Examples are available in: Richard Reschika, *Praxis christlicher Mystik: Einübung von den Wüstenvätern bis zur Gegenwart*, (Freiburg: Herder, 2007), 37.
[251] Cf. Arnold Benz, *Die Zukunft des Universums: Zufall, Chaos, Gott?*, (Düsseldorf: Patmos Verlag, 1997), 63.
[252] John Polkinghorne, *Science and Theology: An Introduction*, (Minneapolis, MN: SPCK/ Fortress Press, 1998), 101.
[253] Richard Reschika, ibid., 37.
[254] Cf. Jörg Bartel, *Denkender Glaube: Unwissenschaftliche Anmerkungen zum Verhältnis von Glaube und Naturwissenschaft*, in: *Theologie für die Praxis, 36.Jg. 2010 Heft 1/2*, (Göttingen: Edition Ruprecht, 2010), 76.

reconciled toward a more complementary view of reality. Furthermore they can recognize that amazement is not only a result of unexplainable miracles but of an aha reaction in view of describable scientific matters which are miraculous in another way. This insight can lead to a wider understanding of miracles which do not exclude but include natural laws; the image of God changes from a God of the gaps to God as ground of being.

INTERACTION:

Performing astronomical observations already includes the interaction of different people. The preparation and implementation of such events is always teamwork. The communication with interested people or groups, the choice of the observation objects, investigation and research of the astronomical data, the check of the astronomical instruments, the preparation of the welcome and introductory speech, the performance of the observation itself and the documentation and evaluation of the meetings – all these activities require the collaboration of different people in the interest group who share their scientific and theological knowledge and expertise.

Interaction also takes place between the interest group and the visitors of the observatory so that hosts and guests learn from each other. This happens at first on a level of the exchange of astronomical knowledge and education. Many groups of pupils and youths come to the observations in order to compensate the cancellation of astronomy lessons at school and use this opportunity for a meaningful leisure time. The interest group of the observatory is actively engaged in making contact with teachers and pupils of the surrounding schools and working with them. In this sense the observatory project shows the interaction of non-Christians and Christians in order to implement social action, especially for the younger generation.

Beyond the educational level, common observations and experience exchange also create deeper interpersonal relationships between people who are interested in astronomy but otherwise have different opinions and worldviews. Christians and non-Christians, secular and churchly groups meet at the observatory, get to know each other and sometimes even become friends. Good interpersonal relationships between people with different worldviews are an important condition for a fruitful interdisciplinary dialogue. This is not surprising because even natural science dealing with the impersonal physical world is always an activity of persons and of a community of scientists and therefore 'personal knowledge'.[255] Careful attention to the personal and relational dimension of the discourse provides an open atmosphere between the dialogue partners, widens mutual understanding, increases the tolerance limit and enables common action for the public good.

**Lectures**

INTERCONNECTION:

Next to astronomical observations public lectures about astronomical and theological subjects are a great opportunity for dialogue between faith and science. These lectures take place in different settings where people who are interest in astronomy and in interdisciplinary dialogue come together. First of all, lectures about astronomy and related topics were offered at the observatory itself as informational units for the visitors immediately before the astronomical observation or as a substitution for an observation when the weather situation hampered the view of the sky. Lectures on special open house days at the astronomical observatory, e.g. on the occasion of the annual "Astronomy Day" or the "Dresdner Long Night of the Sciences" provide a means of dialogue between (hobby-) astronomers and the interested public. Next to these opportunities, the interest group has performed public lectures and informational events at a restaurant near the observatory, at the University of Technology and at city festivals in order to

---

[255] This is the central theory of the physical chemist and philosopher Michael Polany. Cf. the summary of his approach in: John Polkinghorne, *Science and Theology:* 15f.

attract new supporters. Furthermore, celebrations within the interest group (e.g. Christmas parties) or connected to the progress of the observatory project (e.g. inauguration, anniversary celebrations) have mostly included a short lecture about a topic which links astronomical and theological aspects. All these meetings and events with a single lecture or lecture series have brought people with different skills, worldviews and interests together and enabled more specific information and deeper discussion about astronomical and theological subjects than is possible at the normal astronomical observations with random visitors. Empirically, people who have participated in such lectures learned more about astronomy, got interested in related philosophical, theological and ethical questions, and got motivated in continuing the dialogue between faith and science.

The dialogue between natural science and faith has also been established within the congregational program of the Emmaus UMC. Various events and meetings of the congregation have become a platform for lectures, discussions and exchange of arguments. Church services, sermons, church education for children and youths, retreats and small group meetings have addressed the relationship between astronomy and Christian faith. In the congregational context the audience is relatively homogenous and united by the common Christian faith and charismatic spirituality. Here the dialogue takes place not so much by the encounter of people with completely different worldviews or within a pluralistic setting like the meetings at the observatory or in the public. In East Germany with its mostly atheistic society the barrier is relatively high for non-Christians to come to a churchly event. Despite this, the dialogue is also necessary and possible within and with the congregation by dealing with the topic in various ways and discussing the issue on the common ground of Christian faith. There is a great openness but also need for more astronomical and theological knowledge in order to initiate a competent dialogue that will then mostly takes place in daily and professional life. Otherwise there is much knowledge among the church members which is still unused and waiting for activation in order to support this intellectual debate outside the church. The responses and sometimes controversial reactions among the membership show the diversity of opinions and thoughts about this topic and the necessity to equip Christians for the dialogue with non-Christian intellectuals.

INFORMATION:

Lectures are a great opportunity to inform people outside and inside the church in order to create dialogue between astronomy and Christian faith. They enable an intensive communication of scientific and theological knowledge and a more in-depth exchange about it. The setting of a lecture (e.g. as a public lesson, as an inauguration speech or as a sermon in a church service) as well as the profession and the ideological belief of the speaker influence the form and content of the information. This diversity is not an obstacle but an enrichment of the dialogue. The interest group comprises people with knowledge in different fields and practices a division of work regarding the required lectures. For instance, the leader of the interest group undertakes the lectures about the developing and progress of the project, the chronicler speaks about the former history of the observatory, teachers and scientists give lessons about specific astronomical, physical or mathematical subjects, other hobby astronomers introduce the telescopes and astronomical instruments, a woman of letters is an expert of the mythological background of the constellations and my lectures deals with the theological, philosophical and ethical questions. The prepared lectures are available for the members of the interest group as power point presentations on the intranet of the observatory website so that there is a pool of resources which enables intercommunication between lecturers and their specialist fields.

Sometimes the entire potential of knowledge, expertise and capabilities of the interest group is in action when the audience gets informed by a lecture series. Such a special lecture event usually takes place at a public place like a restaurant or a lecture hall and consists of a series of speeches. For instance, a lecture series was focused on the subject "Moon" and included various lessons, e.g. about "The use of the observatory for extracurricular education", "The Moon and its physical and astronomical features", "The Apollo Program", "Astronomical References in the Bible" and "Practical Observations of a Hobby Astronomer".[256] The variety of scientific (astronomical data), theological (biblical references) and ethical (astronautics) information presented by different people of the interest group enables a more complementary picture of the world, opens the horizon of the audience toward other fields and increases the readiness to enter the dialogue.

Profound information about scientific and theological subjects is also very necessary within the church. Even church services can be a platform for the dialogue between faith and natural science amidst a mostly Christian audience. Sermons[257] based on the astronomical references in the Bible, e.g. about worshipping the firmament (Ps 19), the gift of the Sun and the destiny of the Moon (Gn 1:14-19), the lesson of the planets (Jude 13), and the question of theodicy in the light of the starry sky (Job 9:1-11) can connect astronomical knowledge with a spiritual message. The liturgy of the church year also provides a wide range of subjects which are linked to Astronomy. It starts by basic remarks about the nature of time and the structure of the liturgical calendar and goes on by devotions or sermons on different church festivals, e.g about the star of Bethlehem at Christmas, the eclipse of the sun on Good Friday, the rising sun on Easter Sunday, an astronomical breathing exercise at Pentecost[258] and the insight that we are star dust on Eternity Sunday. Furthermore the hymn book includes many songs with metaphorical

[256] See the appendix: Lecture Program
[257] These sermons are available as MP3 files on the website of the Emmaus UMC: http://www.gbz-emmaus.de/predigt-mp3.php
last access: 10 January 2012
[258] Cf. Arnold Benz, ibid., 75ff.

links to celestial bodies like the Sun, Moon and stars[259] which are a fruitful resource for the dialogue about the meaning of astronomy for Christian faith. Another opportunity to make people in the church familiar with the dialogue between faith and natural science is education. Children and youths should already be sufficiently informed in both fields. Therefore the church education of the Emmaus UMC has included various lessons about astronomy in the Bible (e.g. in the creation story), the history of science (e.g. about its beginnings at the monasteries and the conflicts in the modern era), biographies of Christian scientists and astronomers (e.g. about Michael Faraday, Nicolaus Copernicus, Christoph Scheiner) and contemporary projects of the dialogue (e.g. at the astronomical observatory Dresden-Gönnsdorf, and the research facilities of the Jesuits or the Vatican Observatory in Castel Gandolfo and Tucson, Arizona). In addition adult education in the congregation has also dealt with similar subjects. At retreats, bible study meetings and small groups (sometimes involving experts in particular fields) were offered information about the observatory project, the seasonal starry sky, the currently visible astronomical events, the phenomenon of shade and shadow, the atomic structure of the world or the role of intuition in the process of research. All these subjects contain scientific and theological elements even if congregational events are usually more focused on the latter. Contrary to astronomical observations and public lectures about astronomical topics the starting point here is more the theological and spiritual interest which gets a wider understanding by scientific information.

---

[259] In the German hymn book of the UMC there are a wide range of songs with astronomical terms, e.g. "Sun" (48 times), "Moon" (16 times), "Star" or "Stars" (34 times) , and various terms for sky, firmament or outer space – in: Evangelisch-methodistische Kirche in Deutschland, Österreich und Schweiz/Frankreich, *Gesangbuch der Evangelisch-methodistischen Kirche*, (Stuttgart: Medienwerk der Evangelsich-methodistischen Kirche GmbH, 2002)

INTERCHANGE:

Lectures offer a great possibility for the interchange of knowledge and arguments in order create an interesting dialogue. Whereas the strength of astronomical observations is immediate impressions and experiences on the telescopes and personal amazement, lectures better support the critical reflection of a subject within a group. Lectures and following discussions often cause processes of group dynamics which influence the dialogue. According to the make-up of the audience regarding professions and worldviews of the participants it reveals that the dialogue between faith and science also has to deal with the prerogative of interpretation and questions of power. Sometimes it seems that the interchange is more effective in small academic circles or when the dialogue is moderated by people who are competent in both fields. However, a group should be aware of power issues which can disturb the dialogue, especially when there is confusion about the possibilities and limits of religious and scientific interpretation of reality. It is helpful to pay attention to the basic difference that natural science usually describes *how* things are and theological reflections explain *why* or *for what* things are. Even Aristotle distinguished between the efficient cause, which is a description of how the phenomenon takes place, while the final cause is an explanation of the reason or the purpose. Indeed, "one aspect of the scientific revolution of the seventeenth century was that it turned away from the final causes so central to the Aristotelian worldview and concentrated on efficient causes, the how of phenomena."[260] Otherwise, since that time it is clear that the belief in a final cause embodied in a Creator God or the teleological questions for the purpose of the universe does not belong to the field of natural science. The dialogue partners need to recognize that the interchange between religion and natural science can only be fair and on equal footing when the differences and limits of their fields are respected from both sides.

---

[260] Owen Gingerich, ibid., 12. 84.

The participants in this dialogue also have to bear in mind that religion and natural science have differences in the perception of reality and the language they use to express it. Both fields experience and speak about the one reality in different ways: Natural science tries to define the natural world in an objective, impersonal way (even if today it is well known that a researching observer of an experiment is a part of it) while religion deals with the subjective and personal. Whereas natural science uses mostly abstract formulae, equations or models in order to express insights about the world and its order religion speaks on an existential, relational and participating level about God and the world using metaphors and symbols. Even in the case that theology and natural science use the same terms both sides need to be aware of their different meanings (cf. Pannenberg's use of the term "field"). However, acknowledging and taking these differences seriously as two ways of recognizing and describing the world enables us to speak about nature as a scientific object as well as God's creation. Thereby a religious dialogue partner can refer to the fact, that this distinction between the objective and participating view of reality conforms to the Jewish-Christian belief in God's transcendence.[261] God is not an immanent part of the world and thus not an object of natural science. He also doesn't intervene in natural orders but is its transcendent ground and sustainer. Thus the faith in God as creator cannot be questioned by natural science, just like the belief in God cannot criticize natural science by religious arguments. All in all, the goal of the interchange is not to mingle theology and natural science but to relate them in a way that the "how" and the "why" (or "for what"), the objective and the subjective view of reality, the impersonal and personal-participating language come together in a "consonant relationship".[262]

---

[261] Cf. Arnold Benz, ibid., 57.
[262] John Polkinghorne, *Science and Theology:* 21.

INTERACTION:

Lectures about astronomical subjects and related topics enable a wide range of interaction between people with different professions, interests and worldviews. This is already happening within the interest group which represents a mirror image of our pluralistic society. Meetings and celebrations of the interest group sometimes starts with a short lecture by a member who addresses a relevant topic of the dialogue between Christian faith and natural science and invites the group to reflection and discussion. It can be a historical topic, e.g. about news concerning the history of the astronomical observation or a short presentation of a biography of a religious researcher like Max Planck, a seasonally relevant subject, e.g about Christmas and the consequences of the incarnation for extraterrestrial life, or an emerging controversial question, e.g. about the relevance of astrology. These short lectures and the following discussions within the interest group promote the dialogue, common learning and give new ideas for further public lectures. To plan, prepare, perform and evaluate public lectures requires a lot of knowledge and expertise and promote the collaboration between the members of the interest group.

Public lectures convey the dialogue between theology and natural science in society and give a chance to address its ethical and social implications. If Christians speak in the context of public dialogue about the question of God then also social questions are raised. But also science and research don't happen in a vacuum but need to take place in a context of ethical and social responsibility. Therefore the dialogue between religion and science needs to pay attention to the question of who has the power to define social reality and address the ethical and social responsibility of science and research. The well known phrase *knowledge is power* makes Christian and non-Christian intellectuals aware that knowledge and its transfer or exchange is never neutral. Today there is an increasing number of poor and big social differences even in the highly developed societies of Europe and the U.S.[263] Education and qualification of young people in the western countries are more and more a question of class and income.[264] Additionally, the increasing globalization is on the one hand a big chance for knowledge transfer but on the other hand many poor people of the world are excluded from equal chances for education. Thus the dialogue between natural science and religion is not only about the theoretical question of God and the scientific view of the reality in general but also includes a social-ethical component. This insight needs to be addressed by the dialogue between science and theology and has to accomplish this in practical ways. Therefore the observatory project espouses free access for all people, including the poor, to knowledge, education and culture. Subjects of social justice, cultural participation and educational policy play a direct and indirect role in our meetings and lectures. Practically the interest group supplements the astronomy lessons at the schools[265] so that children of socially weak families also have a chance of free extracurricular education. Furthermore the interest group is making contact with another research institute (Helmholtz-Centre Dresden-Rossendorf) in order to create a partnership for educational and extracurricular training. Meanwhile it has started a private lesson project for academically weak pupils at the Emmaus UMC which will provide further interaction between the congregation and the interest group for the public good. Christians and non-Christians have a common social goal and create a coalition for social justice and equal educational chances.

A further area of interaction is the common responsibility for the integrity of creation. The first (East-) German cosmonaut Sigmund Jähn confessed after his spaceflight in 1978: "Before I flew I was already aware of how small and vulnerable our planet is; but only when I saw it from space, in all its ineffable

[263] Cf. Ivan Petrella, *Beyond Liberation Theology: A Polemic*, (London: SCM Press, 2008), 45ff.

[264] Cf. e.g. the publication of the German Bundestag, *Lebenslagen in Deutschland – Dritter Armuts- und Reichtumsbericht*, (Deutscher Bundestag Drucksache 16/9915, 30. 06. 2008).

[265] Since 2007 astronomy is not an obligatory subject at the schools in the federal state Saxony but only a small part of the school subject 'physics'.

beauty and fragility, did I realize that humankind's most urgent task is to cherish and preserve it for future generations."[266] These words of his speech were not published during the GDR regime when churchly peace and environmental groups were hindered and persecuted. But today many people in East Germany are also aware of the responsibility to protect our blue planet earth. We live in one world where not only the scientific and technological progress but also the environmental problems are global. Mahatma Ghandi's insight is true when he stated: "*The earth provides enough to satisfy every man's need, but not every man's greed.*"[267] Currently 86% of the earthly resources are consumed by only 20% of the population in the developed countries and we would need two planets earth by 2050 if all people in the world would live according to the average life standard of US and UK citizens![268] It is obvious that we have to renew our relationship with nature as God's creation. Theologically, nature is one of the great texts of God and his first sacrament revealing his life, creativity and beauty. "When we forget our fundamental connection to the earth we lose something of ourselves."[269] We are called to responsible stewardship which is one major aspect of participation in God's sustaining and redeeming activity in the world. The astronomical observatory project is an attempt to give people an idea of the greatness and beauty of the universe. Observations of the starry sky and public lectures make people aware how many astronomical conditions were necessary so that life could emerge on Earth. People are often awed and become thankful for the gift of life. They get motivated to protect the environment after experiencing nature as a wonderful creation. The dialogue between science and theology is necessary in order to remind us of our creational bonds with the Earth and to develop ethical values for sustaining and protecting our environment. Otherwise the destruction of nature could

---

[266] Daniel E. Groody, *Globalization, Spirituality, and Justice*, (New York, NY: Maryknoll, 2010), 2.
[267] Quotation in: Daniel E. Groody, ibid., 11.
[268] Human Development Report 1998, quoted in: Daniel E. Groody, ibid., 257.
[269] Daniel E. Groody, 256.

also increase violence within society. The dialogue contributes to an understanding of science within a larger context of creation by a loving God and helps theology to take into account results of natural science in order to confess a contemporary theology of creation. A renewed relation to creation, supported by natural science, can also help the church to rediscover the "liturgy of creation". Pierre Teilhard De Chardin's "The Mass on the World"[270] considers the celebration of the Eucharist as the heart of the transformation of the created world by the Spirit of God. It is about the consecration of the whole world, the diaphany of all created things – in short: a universal communion.[271]

The astronomical observatory project is a realm where the *power of participation*[272] becomes practised and exercised. This power of participation calls upon all people as images of God to be His servants in this world and take part in His life-sustaining and redeeming activity.[273] Christians and non-Christians speak together about the common responsibility for the blue planet Earth, learn from each other how to implement it practically and communicate this important issue to the public. The group also takes concrete action, e.g. by planning an eco-friendly construction of a meeting building next to the astronomical observatory or planting an animal-friendly hedge. Considering the extensive environmental pollution, species extinction and climate change in our time the challenge of the survival of further generations can only be met as a common effort. The astronomical observatory project is a great possibility to build a bridge between a religious and a non-religious public for a common ecological goal. Also in this respect it is not only a mission *for* others but *with* others in order to fulfil God's mission in our world.

---

[270] Quoted in: Daniel E. Groody, 256.

[271] Gotthard Fuchs, *Messe über die Welt,* in: *Das Herz des Universums-Einstein und die Frage nach Gott*, Extra-Heft: Christ in der Gegenwart, (Freiburg: Herder, 2005), 23.

[272] Cf. Michael Nausner, Lecture on Leadership in the Context of Global and Intimate Power, Oslo 5 August 2011, transcript

[273] Ibid.

**The Survey**

INTERCONNECTION:

An interesting and effective instrument of the dialogue between religion and natural science was the taking and analysis of a survey[274]. It had helped to involve more people in the dialogue, arouse their interest in the observatory project and use the insights for evaluation. The survey provided the possibility that people could reflect on the relevant subjects more thoroughly and were able to contribute directly but anonymously to the discourse. The informed consent issues were observed and written on the survey form.

In the beginning the survey functioned like a virtual platform for the discourse between people who usually would never come in contact with each other. But the realisation of the survey, the encouraging reactions beyond the simple answering of the survey form and the further evaluation have been a great source for new relationships and networks between people who are interested in the dialogue for various reasons.

The survey was performed from November 2011 till January 2012. Altogether 55 people took part in the survey. Most of them are parishioners and friends of the Emmaus UMC, members and adherents of the interest group and visitors of the astronomical observatory. Among the participants were 47 percent Methodists, 19 percent Lutherans, 8 percent members of non specified denominations, 2 percent Catholics, 2 percent theists and 12 percent atheists; 10 percent didn't state any worldview. This shows that the survey reflects mostly the opinions and beliefs of Christians but also of the relatively well represented atheists even if their number is much higher in East Germany. In view of the professions of the participants, 30 percent work or study in the field of natural sciences and engineering, 20 percent in the field of human sciences and related faculties, 11 percent work in administration, 9 percent work in social professions, 7 percent are craftsmen, 7 percent are entrepreneurs, 7 percent are retired, 5 percent are pupils

[274] See the appendix: Survey Form

(Gymnasium) and 4 percent are not specified. In this way the survey mirrors the great variety of competence and expertise among the participants and reveals the high intellectual level of the dialogue. Regarding the age of the participants, 5 percent were under 18 years, 9 percent between 19 and 30 years, 24 percent between 31 and 45 years, 30 percent between 46 and 59 years, 22 percent over 60 years; and 10 percent declared no age. This shows that a balanced average of age is represented in the survey even if the middle age has the majority. All in all these data display adequately the setting where the dialogue takes place: it is a loose network of people with different ages, beliefs and competences who are also linked to different social organisations and institutions with an educational background. It is our hope that the survey participants will be motivated to continue the dialogue between religion and natural science in various ways.

INFORMATION and INTERCHANGE:

The questions on the survey depict a cross section of the subjects which became relevant through the observatory project. The list of questions was developed by myself in consultation with Prof. Dr. Christoph Metzner who works as a scientist at the Fraunhofer Institute for Electron Beam and Plasma Technology FEP in Dresden. He is an active member of the interest group and familiar with the dialogue between Christian faith and natural science for many years. The following list is a mix of yes-no questions and open questions which participants could answer in as much detail as they desired:

**1. Would you advocate a strict separation of religion and natural science? Yes/ No. Discuss your answer.**

This question wanted to find out the participants' view of the general relationship between religion and natural science. Two-thirds (66 percent) of the participants answered this question with No, only one-third (34 percent) said Yes. The added explanations of the respondents showed that the participants were quite aware that the question was not about the different methodology of theology and natural science which need to be distinguished. So the vote is indeed a strong affirmation that both fields need to be linked. The participants' worldview or religion did not seem to play a significant role in their answer to this question. Atheists and Christians were in almost equal proportions among the opponents and proponents of a separation of religion and natural science. Interestingly more people who work in the field of natural science or related fields were against a separation than people who work in humanities. All in all this represents a positive result revealing a growing openness and readiness to support a relationship between religion and natural science. Of course, the nature of relationship (e.g. partnership, dialogue, integration, assimilation...) was not a part of this question.

**2. Would you claim that natural science can completely describe the reality of the world and the universe? Yes/ No. If not, what entities or authorities would come into question?**

This question alluded to a claim of the former communist ideology in East-Germany which considered the view of natural science as the only one which can define reality. Many participants still know the ideological indoctrination of that time. But the result of the survey is very clear: 89 percent said No to such a claim, only 9 percent said Yes and 2 percent couldn't give an answer. It is interesting to note that those who answered Yes were half and half, atheists and believers. It is surprising that half of the Christians consider natural science capable of completely describing reality, but maybe this has to do with a narrow understanding of the term "reality". A special dependence of the answers based on the profession of the participants was not visible. The majority concedes that natural science is a very important way of describing the world but not the only one. Human sciences, religion and arts were mentioned as other fields which are necessary in order to get a more complete picture of the reality of the world and the universe.

**3. Would you say that the research findings of natural science prove that God does not exist? Yes/ No.**

The third question is connected to the second one and led to a similar response: 91 percent wouldn't say that scientific insights contradict the existence of God, but 9 percent claim the opposite. Of course, the latter position is only represented by atheists, independent of their profession. But only one-third of the atheistic participants gave such an answer, two-thirds of them were not convinced that natural science proves the non-existence of God! This again would mean that the majority of the atheistic participants agree that atheism is not a consequence of natural science but a chosen worldview. They obviously have a differentiated way of looking at things and distinguish science and worldview. Natural science and atheism are not coercively related as adherents as New Atheism claims. On the other hand, Christians need to acknowledge that natural science cannot prove the existence of God. God cannot be a research object of natural science or a part of natural laws; furthermore, God is the condition of their possibility.

**4. While working with astronomy or taking part in an astronomical observation did you ever ask yourself philosophical, theological or ethical questions? Yes/ No. If yes, what kinds of questions you asked?**

This issue arises especially from the observatory project and bases on the experience that dealing with astronomy and astronomical observation trigger mostly hermeneutical questions. Indeed, 82 percent answered Yes but only 18 percent said No. The majority of Christians and almost all atheistic participants stated that they have asked philosophical, theological and ethical questions during or after activities related to astronomy. Among those answering Yes were a significant number of people who study, work or teach in the field of natural science and engineering. This group probably shows a higher responsiveness and capability to cross the boundaries of their fields than others. People who answered Yes mentioned a wide range of questions which arise from dealing with astronomy. The series of questions written by the respondents tended to follow a certain pattern: It started with a desire for a deeper understanding of scientific issues (e.g. of the big bang and big crunch or other cosmologies, of the size and expansion of the universe, of the features of time and space, of the conditions of life, and of the possibility of extraterrestrial life), to philosophical questions (e.g. about the existence of something rather than nothing, the relation between contingency and necessity, the role of intelligence and consciousness), or theological subjects (e.g. about the creation and the action of a Creator God, the whence and whither of life, the meaning of human existence, the universal salvation, the relation between natural laws and God's action, the end of the world) and finally to ethical subjects (e.g. about the responsibility of human beings as the summit of creation, the environmental and life protection on our blue planet Earth, benefit and nonsense of spaceflights and extraterrestrial activities). The term "amazement" emerges very often regarding astronomical topics and actually seems to be the meeting point between natural science and existential questions.

**5. Who is in your opinion responsible for answering of questions regarding the meaning and values of life or ethical subjects?**

This question asks for the persons and institutions which have the right and the authority to define values and decide ethical issues. Everybody who answered saw the necessity of such entities which give orientation in questions of meaning or provide an ethical framework. Of course, the opinion who or what is responsible for existential and ethical questions is deeply divided among the participants and essentially depends on their worldview. Most atheists answered that all people are autonomous in defining ethical standards and values. But also the philosophy, social institutions, politics and even church and religion were considered as responsible for ethics and the communication of values. Christians stated strongly that religion is responsible for ethical issues and mentioned that God, the Bible and the church have the main authority to give binding orientation. They emphasized much less the role of one's own conscience, the philosophy or the social institutions in this respect. The participants' professional background seemed to play no significant role in their answer to this question. Altogether it can be stated that all participants recognize that there are various ways of existential and ethical orientation. Independent of their ideological and professional background they are aware that natural science and research need an ethical framework because they don't develop ethical standards and values by themselves. This consensus shows that ethical questions regarding the human accountability for the preservation of our planet are an important topic of the dialogue between religion and science.

**6. Is the worldview of a scientist important for you? Yes/ No. When a scientist comments on ideological or ethical issues how much do you value their statements?**

This question arises from the observation that nowadays some scientists publicly espouse particular worldviews (cf. New Atheism, Creationism). It should find out if the professional reputation influences his or her credibility regarding ideological or ethical statements and vice versa. Anyway, over two-thirds (69 percent) are interested in the worldview of a scientist, almost one-third (28 percent) see no relevance; the remainder is uncertain (3 percent). This result is almost the same among Christians and Atheists. Interesting is the difference between participants who work in the fields of natural science and engineering and those who works in the fields of human sciences. Whereas among the first-mentioned over two-third stated a relevance of the worldview, the latter answered almost half and half. People of other professions also share the higher interest in the worldview like the natural scientists do. This shows the relatively high importance of the worldview or religion of a scientist and the sensibility of the audience in this regard, especially among natural scientists themselves. In general it should be clear that a scientist always has a worldview even if natural science doesn't involve it methodically (although in some fields, e.g. regarding the different cosmologies, the research seems to be influenced by ideological perspectives too). When a scientist takes a stand on philosophical, religious and ethical topics it would be fair to make it clear in what capacity the statement is made. Insights of the natural sciences can inform philosophical, theological or ethical debates and make both fields more consonant with each other. Insofar scientific and ideological statements can be correlated in a good way but they shouldn't be mingled methodically.

**7. Should theology regard and include insights of natural science and involve them in its statements? Yes/ No. To what extent must statements of faith be provable by experience like in natural scientific observations?**

The first part of the issue asks for the relationship between theology and natural science regarding theology's adoption of scientific insights and findings. The overwhelming majority (80 percent) plead in favour of an openness of theology toward insights of the natural sciences. Only a fifth (20 percent) is sceptical and said No. Among the atheistic participants the percentage is proportionately exactly the same. Thereby the proponents understand it more as a critical call toward religion to be more consonant with modern sciences, while the opponents fear again an inappropriate mingling of both fields. The high percentage of Christians who support an intensive adoption of scientific insights is surprising, at least among the membership of the Emmaus UMC. In the past the relationship between theology and natural science has been seen more critically in the congregation even among members who work in scientific or technical fields. In the survey the latter have voted exactly half and half for and against an adoption of findings while over 90 percent of people working in fields of human sciences were in favour of it. All in all this result shows a great openness for the dialogue between Christian faith and natural science, probably not least by the influence of the observatory project. But there is also a sceptical attitude among Christian natural scientists which needs to be addressed in the future.

The second issue was not answerable by Yes and No and aimed for the role of experience in the area of religion and natural science. Christians emphasize that religion is mostly linked with experiences of faith, and even atheists don't deny such statement. But both sides also expresses the awareness that experience in religion and in natural science has different meanings. In the first area it has personal, subjective and relational character, is usually not always repeatable, and cannot 'prove' God's existence. In the second field experience can play a role regarding scientific observations and experiments but needs to be objective, repeatable under the same conditions and describable by natural laws and theories. Although religious statements are not provable by the latter understanding of experience, they can still be true. This was widely confirmed especially by participants who are active in the field of human sciences or arts which steer a middle course. But the audience agreed that human reason needs to be at work in all fields even if in different ways.

**8. Are natural orders in your opinion always and everywhere valid? Yes/ No. Do you believe in miracles and how do you define them?**

This issue should clarify the relation between natural laws and God's action, particularly exemplified by the understanding of miracles. The audience was in disagreement about the first question: 36 percent answered Yes and confirmed the omnicausality of natural laws; 62 percent said No and assume exceptions, and the remainder was undecided. Almost all atheists suppose that natural laws are everywhere and always effective without exceptions; Christians usually don't agree on such statement. Interesting is the response of natural scientists and related professions regarding the natural laws: 86 percent answer No and see the validity of natural laws limited, only 14 percent say Yes and state no limits. In comparison, 56 percent of the people working in human sciences and related fields answered No and 44 percent Yes. The reason for the different result could be that people who deal with natural sciences see more clearly the problem behind the issue. For instance, they refer to the fact that natural laws are by definition limited to described realms or conditions and explain only a part of the reality. Their validity 'always' and 'everywhere' is not provable in the whole universe – both spatial and temporal (e.g. immediately after the big bang). Additionally their description needs to be falsifiable which means that they are revisable and maybe terminable.

The second question regarding miracles and their definition is partially dependent on the answer of the first one, especially when a miracle is defined as an invalidation of natural laws. In this meaning most of the atheists deny a belief in miracles. But in a very general meaning (e.g. regarding the unique conditions of life on the Earth) or as subjective experience of fulfilment of a very unexpected event 55 percent of them believe in miracles! The overwhelming majority of Christians tend to believe in miracles, mostly understood as (single) cancellations of natural laws. But their explanations also show a great awareness that the belief in miracles is mostly a subjective experience and belongs to the realm of religion and not of natural science.

Interesting again is the reflection of the issue according to the professional background of the audience. Participants working in fields of natural science and related professions believe mostly in miracles understood as a breach of natural laws (81 percent) while the remainder see the real cause of miracles in the limitation of human perception in general or the lack of present scientific knowledge. In comparison, only 27 percent of people working in the fields of human sciences and arts believe in miracles as suspending natural laws, the others understand miracles mostly grounded in subjective experiences. In the end it is surprising that only less than 10 percent of all participants deny expressively any belief in miracles. The dialogue about the conditions of natural laws and the understanding of miracles seems to be a fruitful topic between science and religion. Thereby the Christian side needs to be aware that God is not only seen as a stopgap which fills the gaps of human knowledge. Such God of the gaps can be dispensable very fast by new scientific insights. Furthermore, God should be understood as always acting by the continuous creation and the contingency of all occurrences, including natural laws. Then the continuity of the latter can be understood as a wonderful expression of God's faithfulness (cf. Pannenberg).

**9. How do judge the relationship between religion and natural science throughout history and at the presence? Can you undergird your position by an example?**

This question asks for the participants' view of the history and present of the relationship between Christian faith and natural science or research. Almost all participants independent of their worldview or profession judge the past relationship between religion and natural science as negative. They begin the reply mostly with the struggles between both sides in the modern time and describe the following period as characterized by competition, rivalry, tensions, hostility and antagonism. Thereby they emphasize with reason the failures of the church which ignored new scientific insights or even persecuted scientists. As negative examples are mentioned Galileo Galilei, Nicolai Copernicus, Giordano Bruno and Johannes Kepler. Some participants add that the struggles were not so much caused by the opposition of religion and science itself but by power struggles.

The evaluation of the present relationship between religion and science is much more differentiated across the audience. Independent of worldview or profession it is described as mutual ignorance, friendly coexistence but mostly as an attempt of usurpation by the one or the other side. Atheists mostly emphasize that religion and theology need to be consonant with natural science. Christians (including the majority of Christian scientists!) often complain that science would become a surrogate religion (e.g. by statements of scientists of the New Atheism movement or fundamentalist Evolutionism and social Darwinism) but see also critically that religious fundamentalists manipulate natural science (Creationism). But the conflict areas seem to be more between religion and biology rather than between religion and physics or chemistry so that the field of astronomy is less affected. Altogether it looks like there is still much to do for a fruitful dialogue; for instance, accounting for the past which would include intensive analysis of the history of the conflict (which was quite different regarding the involved denominations and affected countries), an open confession of guilt and a commitment to reconciliation and fair discourse. Then people would reach the insight that the history of the relationship between religion and science is much richer than their struggles. Here it could be refer to the biblical demythologized understanding of creation which is one source of modern natural science, the rich tradition of monasteries which originally connected spirituality and nature study, and not least to the many Christian scientists in the past and present who connect their faith with their profession. Maybe then a new re-narration of the history of science would be in sight.

**10. How can the dialogue between natural science and religion get initiated or intensified? What do you wish in this respect from the dialogue partners?**

The last question is about the ideas of the audience in order to support the dialogue between religion and science and to specify the expectations from those who take part in it. First, the overwhelming majority of the answering participants welcome a dialogue - independent on worldview or profession. Only very few people were more sceptical regarding its necessity or success. The respondents mostly wrote about the necessary attitude of the dialogue partners and the basic conditions of the discourse. They state that only mutual openness, tolerance, fairness and respect lead to a fruitful dialogue. Furthermore, dialogue at eye level requires readiness to learn more from other fields and to acknowledge the limits of one's own methods and subject areas. It would be also helpful to name purpose and goal of the dialogue and speak openly about power issues in order to reduce their unconscious influence and the misuse of the prerogative interpretation. The polled wished that the dialogue lead to more knowledge exchange which generates an increasing consonance between religion and science. Additionally, it should have a significant ethical component addressing the ethical framework of science and research, the responsibility for the life of future generations and the commitment of all fields for common good. The observatory project and its activities like astronomical observations, public lectures and discussions and maybe future publications are seen as a great chance and opportunity to bring forward the dialogue between intellectuals with various expertise and beliefs.

INTERACTION:

The survey has provided a lot of interaction. Like already mentioned its preparation and performance connected different people, increased the interest in the observatory project and pushed the dialogue into a wider public. The response to the survey was very encouraging and the results are very valuable for further evaluation and future activities. The effort and expertise of the participants who often answered the questions in much detail and with passion deserve to present and work with the results in meetings of the interest group, public lectures, professional discussions, and churchly events. Even a series of thematic sermons about the answered topics is imaginable. Except for the observatory project the dialogue between religion and science will primarily go on in the setting of small groups and coteries as a proxy dialogue in the hope that more and more intellectuals in Dresden -

Christian and non-Christian - get interested in it and implement it in their professional and churchly environment. Anyway, Christian faith in the Triune God can contribute very well to such dialogue by living the Trinitarian love as a model of mutual interconnectedness, equal access to information, fair interchange and common interaction.

**Summary: The Goal of the Dialogue**

An important issue at the end of this chapter and of the whole dissertation is to ask for the purpose and goal of the dialogue between Christian faith and natural science. The necessity of such a dialogue in Dresden has become obvious: Amidst a highly secularized society in East Germany the church cannot withdraw back into a pious ghetto but needs to be a part of the important public discourse about the role of natural science and research. A contextual theology-in this case a theology in the context of natural science - is greatly required today. The belief in the Trinitarian God gives orientation in this discourse, first for the believers themselves who study, teach and work in these fields and who want to link faith and profession. But it also has social and global relevance when the question of the ethical framework of science and research or of our responsibility for the future of our planet is raised. However, the primary purpose of the dialogue cannot be an apologetical concern in order to increase the public influence of Christian doctrines or of the church in order to acquire new adherents and members among scientists and related professions. Rather the dialogue has its purpose in itself and aims for a common mission *with* others for a better understanding of our world and human destiny. For that reason Christians should not behave as people who demand the prerogative interpretation but enter the dialogue as learning partners whose faith can contribute to a more complementary understanding of complex reality. This also means that the goal of dialogue is not assimilation from the one or the other side. Natural science should not attempt to assimilate religion by considering theology as a part of physics, for instance, nor should religion try to incorporate physics or astronomy as a part of theology. Every field has its own subject area and needs to be methodically independent without being isolated or competing with the other. The more the partners are aware of the differences the more they can discover commonalities and are able to create a complementary relationship which leads to growing congruence and consonance of the differing answers of theology and science.[275] An example of the commonality of religion and science is the search for truth or "motivated belief"[276] in order to describe and explain the one complex world. On the one hand theology does not require an act of intellectual suicide but looks for evidence of its doctrines. And on the other hand science cannot completely escape the circularity of experiment and interpretation but is always personal knowledge which includes creativity and intuition. Thus both fields deal with motivated belief and work in a mode of "critical realism"[277] in the common search for truth. Like Anselm of Canterbury said: *Credo ut intelligam* (Proslogion, 1) – I believe so that I may understand – and also knew its correlation: *fides quaerens intellectum* – faith seeking understanding. This dialectical insight perhaps also motivated the magi on their long journey. They found what they searched. At the crèche estranged siblings who belong together came together: science and faith. But we are still on the way there. The way is rocky but the goal cannot be far because: ***We saw his star in the East and have come to worship him.*** (Matthew 2:2)

---

[275] Cf. John Polkinghorne, *Theology in the Context of Science*: 67.
[276] Ibid., 84ff.
[277] John Polkinghorne, *Science and Theology:* 16; and in: *Theology in the Context of Science*: 17.

## APPENDIX

The following materials represent only a little part of official papers, public statements, correspondence with sponsors, minutes of observations or events and etc. But it may give an impression of the comprehensive and divers work of the observatory project and the related dialogue.

**<u>Flyers</u>**

*Sternwarte Gönnsdorf – ein neues Freizeitprojekt des Vereins zur Förderung der Jugend e.V.*

*Historie*

Die Sternwarte Gönnsdorf wurde 1973 von der TU Dresden gebaut. Seit einigen Jahren steht sie ungenutzt. Da dieses Gebäude ein Wahrzeichen im Schönfelder Hochland ist, sollte sie unbedingt erhalten bleiben und einer sinnvollen Nutzung zugeführt werden. Deshalb wurde die Sternwarte im Januar 2009 vom Verein zur Förderung der Jugend e.V. erworben. Dieser bemüht sich besonders um eine vielfältige, niveauvolle und interessante Freizeitgestaltung der Kinder und Jugendlichen im Schönfelder Hochland.

*Künftige Nutzung*

Die Sternwarte soll vorrangig den Schülern der umliegenden Schulen wie Mittelschule Weißig, Gymnasium Bühlau, Grundschulen als außerschulische Weiterbildung dienen, aber auch Hobbyastronomen und interessierten Bürgern als Kommunikationsstätte offen stehen, um auf diese Weise die älteste Naturwissenschaft „Astronomie" allen Interessierten näher zu bringen. Live-Beobachtungen sowie Diavorträge werden daher ein fester Bestandteil der Nutzung sein.

*Was ist zu tun?*

Die Sternwarte ist z. Zt. völlig entkernt, d.h. ohne Medienanschlüsse und muss als Erstes von Grund auf saniert werden. Eine echte Herausforderung ist die Sanierung der Kuppel. Danach folgen die Inneneinrichtung und die Ausstattung mit optischen/technischen Geräten. Aber auch die Außenanlage soll dem Anliegen entsprechend gestaltet werden. Jedoch geht es nicht ohne Ihre Unterstützung. Wir benötigen unbedingt Verbündete, die uns finanziell und/oder materiell helfen, unser Ziel zu erreichen.

*Unser Ziel*

„Das Weltall – Du lebst darin, entdecke es" ist das Motto des diesjährigen Internationalen Jahres der Astronomie. Wir haben uns deshalb das anspruchsvolle Ziel gesetzt, die Sternwarte bis Ende des Jahres 2009 wenigstens „startklar" zu machen. Die im April 2009 gegründete Interessengemeinschaft „Sternwarte Gönnsdorf", der u.a. Hobbyastronomen, Sternenfreunde, Lehrer sowie interessierte Bürger angehören, ist voller Tatendrang.

*Kontaktdaten*

Verein zur Förderung der Jugend e.V.
Ansprechpartner: Renate Franz
E-Mail: rfranz@sternwarte-goennsdorf.de
Telefon: 03 51 / 2 68 12 72

Unser Spendenkonto: Ostsächsische Sparkasse Dresden
BLZ 850 503 00
Konto-Nr. 3 120 055 963
Verwendungszweck: Sternwarte Gönnsdorf

*Wir danken dem HochlandVerlag Pappritz, der uns den Druck dieses Flyers sponsert.*

Aus einer alten hässlichen Hülle wurde eine wunderschöne „Lady“ die

# STERNWARTE DRESDEN-GÖNNSDORF

Saniert im
Internationalen Jahr der Astronomie 2009

www.sternwarte-goennsdorf.de

...und das ist das Ergebnis des unermüdlichen Engagements der Interessengemeinschaft „Sternwarte Dresden-Gönnsdorf“, die sich vor einem Jahr gegründet hat.

*Was geschah seit der Gründung im April 2009?*

Innerhalb eines Jahres konnten wir mit Unterstützung von Sponsoren – den mittleren und kleineren Gewerbetreibenden aus dem Schönfelder Hochland – die bauliche Sanierung der Sternwarte voranbringen. Aber auch Firmen aus Dresden und Pirna hatten ein Herz für unser Projekt. Unzählige Eigenleistungen der IG Mitglieder wurden erbracht. Und nicht zuletzt haben uns die Geldspenden ein Stück weitergeholfen. Auch einige optische Geräte sind bereits vorhanden.

Unser Ziel, die Sternwarte zu einem niveauvollen und attraktiven Freizeitprojekt für Kinder und Jugendliche auszubauen, gehen wir zielstrebig an. So planen wir nach Beendigung der baulichen Voraussetzungen ab Herbst 2010 zweimal in der Woche, Dienstag und Mittwoch, die Betreuung von Schülern. Die Zusammenarbeit mit Grundschulen, der Mittelschule Weißig, Berthold-Brecht-Gymnasium sowie dem Gymnasium Bühlau hat bereits begonnen. Aber auch für Hobbyastronomen und interessierte Bürger soll die Sternwarte ein Anziehungspunkt werden. Neben der Beobachtung von Himmelskörpern bei klarem Himmel soll bei schlechtem Wetter Theorie in Form von Vorträgen vermittelt werden. Dafür werden zur Zeit die entsprechenden Rahmenbedingungen erarbeitet.

Unsere Suche nach staatlicher Förderung blieb bis heute erfolglos. So sind wir weiterhin auf Spenden angewiesen. Denn viele Arbeiten stehen noch aus und unser großer Traum, ein 16"-Teleskop, steht zurzeit förmlich in den Sternen.

Wir würden uns freuen, wenn Sie uns finanziell oder materiell unterstützen könnten. Wenn Sie unser Projekt interessiert, dann besuchen Sie uns doch einmal auf unserer Homepage www.sternwarte-goennsdorf.de

Selbstverständlich können Sie auch telefonisch oder persönlich Kontakt mit uns aufnehmen

*Kontaktdaten*

Verein zur Förderung der Jugend e.V.

| | |
|---|---|
| Ansprechpartner | Renate Franz |
| E-Mail | rfranz@sternwarte-goennsdorf.de |
| Telefon | 03 51/2 68 12 72 |
| *Unser Spendenkonto* | Ostsächsische Sparkasse Dresden |
| | BLZ 850 503 00 |
| | Konto-Nr. 3 120 055 963 |
| | Verwendungszweck: Sternwarte Gönnsdorf |

Die Herstellung des Flyers erfolgte mit freundlicher Unterstützung des HochlandVerlag Pappritz

## Rules of Operation – Attachment 6

**Anlage 6** zur Betriebsordnung der IG Sternwarte Dresden-Gönnsdorf

**Nutzung der Sternwarte Gönnsdorf**

als niveauvolles Freizeitangebot vorrangig für Kinder und Jugendliche des Schönfelder Hochlandes zur außerschulischen Bildung

- Nutzung durch die **„Sternegucker AG"** der Mittelschule Weißig

- Nutzung durch **Schulen** der Umgebung wie Mittelschule Weißig, Gymnasium Bühlau und weiterer schulischer Einrichtungen

- Einbeziehung der Grundschulen und Kindergärten zur **naturwissenschaftlichen Vorbildung**

- Nutzung für außerschulische Projekte und Arbeitsgemeinschaften innerhalb der Ganztagesangebote

- Nutzung für **Neigungskurse** und spezielle Inhalte des Physikunterrichtes z.B. Beobachtungsaufgaben: **Mond, Planeten, Galaxien, Kugelsternhaufen, offene Sternhaufen, außergewöhnliche Sternhaufen und Kometen**

- **Begegnungs- und Kommunikationsstätte** für Hobbyastronomen und interessierte Bürger, um auf diese Weise die älteste Naturwissenschaft „Astronomie" allen Interessierten näher zu bringen. **Die Sternwarte soll Menschen mit unterschiedlichen Weltanschauungen zusammenführen und dem Dialog zwischen Naturwissenschaft und Philosophie dienen.**

- **Live-Beobachtungen** und **Vorträge** rund um die Astronomie werden ein fester Bestandteil der Nutzung sein.

- **Die Raumfahrt** ist ein weiteres interessantes Thema der außerschulischen Bildung

- Die Sternwarte soll als Zentrum eines künftigen **Planetenwanderweges** touristisches Ziel im Schönfelder Hochland werden.

## Inauguration Speech

Sehr verehrte Damen und Herren, liebe Gäste!

Mir kommt heute die ehrenvolle Aufgabe zu, die neu renovierte Sternwarte Dresden-Gönnsdorf einzuweihen. Zugegeben ein nicht alltäglicher Akt, dass ein Pastor zu einem solchen Anlass tätig wird, bin ich doch sonst eher für Taufen, Trauungen und Beerdigungen zuständig. Dass ich hier stehe, verdanke ich zum einen meinem Hobby Astronomie, dass mich seit der Schulzeit fasziniert und inspiriert hat: Muss nicht jeder staunen, wenn er an die gigantischen Weiten des Alls denkt und was sich da draußen noch verbergen mag? Oder dass unser blauer Planet sich am Äquator mit 465m/s um sich selbst dreht und uns nicht schwindlig wird? Oder wir jetzt mit ca. 30km/s um die Sonne jagen wie in einem großen Raumschiff, das sich Erde nennt? Freilich, mit dem Himmel habe ich es als Theologe auch sonst zu tun, wobei ich sehr wohl um den Unterschied zwischen dem Universum und der transzendenten Welt Gottes weiß, der in der englischen Sprache präziser mit den zwei Begriffen „sky" und „heaven" ausgedrückt wird.

Beides, der Bereich der Wissenschaft und der Bereich der Theologie haben gewiss ihre je eigenen Grundlagen, Sachgebiete und Methoden, die man nicht einfach vermischen darf. Die freie Forschung kommt sicher ohne die hypothetische Annahme eines göttlichen Wesens aus. Das hat Kirche in ihrer Geschichte manchmal missachtet und so zur verhängnisvollen Entfremdung zwischen Glaube und Wissenschaft beigetragen. Andererseits gehören Glaube und Wissenschaft, Geist und Verstand zusammen, denn wir Menschen fragen nicht nur wissenschaftlich, was die Welt im Innersten zusammenhält, sondern sind auch Wesen, die nach dem Ursprung, Sinn und Ziel des Lebens in geistlicher Hinsicht fragen, worauf die Wissenschaft, wenn sie sich ihrer methodischen Grenzen bewusst bleibt, keine Antwort geben kann. Bezüglich der Sinnfrage und der Ethik hat einer mal pointiert formuliert:

„Antworten kommen nicht von den Sternen. Aber vom Himmel“ (Gemeint ist hier der göttliche Himmel.)

Beim Thema Astronomie spüren wir wohl beides: die Trennung zwischen Wissenschaft und Glaube und ihre Zusammengehörigkeit. Wir schauen immer mit Augen und Verstand aber ebenso mit dem Herzen zum Himmel auf! Immanuel Kant schrieb in seiner „Kritik der Praktischen Vernunft“: "Zwei Dinge erfüllen das Gemüt mit immer neuer und zunehmender Bewunderung und Ehrfurcht, je öfter und anhaltender sich das Nachdenken damit beschäftigt: Der gestirnte Himmel über mir und das moralische Gesetz in mir."

Möge diese Sternwarte beides sein: Ort des Wissens und des Lernens für alle Generationen und Ort des Staunens, des Philosophierens und Glaubens. Ort der Begegnung von Gleichgesinnten, die das Thema und Hobby Astronomie zusammenführt, aber auch ein Ort der Toleranz, wo Menschen unterschiedlicher Weltanschauung, Glaubensrichtung oder sozialer Herkunft zusammenfinden. Ort der Freizeitbeschäftigung und Entspannung und Ort der Bildung eines Bewusstseins der Verantwortung für unseren blauen Planeten und für folgende Generationen.

In diesem Sinne weihe ich diese Sternwarte ein.

Dazu lese ich aus der Bibel einige Verse aus Psalm 8, wo ein Mensch vor ca. 3000 Jahren unter dem Sternhimmel steht und über die Größe Gottes staunt, der sowohl das All als auch uns kleine Menschen geschaffen hat:

Herr, unser Herrscher! Groß und herrlich ist dein Name. Himmel und Erde sind Zeichen deiner Macht. Ich blicke zum Himmel und sehe, was deine Hände geschaffen haben; den Mond und die Sterne - allen hast du ihre Bahnen vorgezeichnet. Was ist da schon der Mensch, dass du an ihn denkst? Wie klein und unbedeutend ist er, und doch kümmerst du dich um ihn. Ja, du hast ihm eine hohe Stellung gegeben - nur wenig niedriger als die Engel. Mit Ruhm und Ehre hast du ihn gekrönt. Du hast ihm den Auftrag gegeben, über deine Geschöpfe zu herrschen. Alles hast du ihm zu Füßen gelegt... Herr, unser Herrscher! Groß und herrlich ist dein Name. Himmel und Erde sind Zeichen deiner Macht.

Gott der Schöpfer lasse diese Sternwarte einen Ort gemeinsamen Lernens, begeisterten Austauschs, interessanter Begegnungen und neu erwachende Verantwortung für unseren blauen Planeten sein. Er halte schützend seine Hände über diesen Ort und segne alle Menschen, die hierher kommen.

Der Herr segne und behüte uns. Der Herr lasse sein Angesicht leuchten über uns und sei uns gnädig. Er erhebe sein Angesicht auf uns und schenke uns Frieden. Amen

Werner Philipp

## Logo

STERNWARTE
DRESDEN
GÖNNSDORF

## Funding-Letters

Verein
zur
Förderung
der
Jugend e.V.

Pillnitzer Str. 21c | 01328 Dresden / OT Weißig
(0351) 217 66 30
(0351) 217 66 31
vorstand@kjhpep.de

Dresden, den 03.04.2009

### „Sternwarte Gönnsdorf"

**ein neues Freizeitangebot im Schönfelder Hochland**

Der Verein zur Förderung der Jugend e.V. ist bestrebt, den Kindern und Jugendlichen im Schönfelder Hochland und der Umgebung niveauvolle Freizeitangebote anzubieten. Ein neues, aber noch nicht nutzbares Projekt ist die Sternwarte Gönnsdorf. Sie ist seit Januar 2009 Eigentum des Vereins und soll nun mit Leben erfüllt werden.

Wie soll die Sternwarte genutzt werden?

Die Sternwarte soll in erster Linie der außerschulischen Weiterbildung der Mittelschüler von Weißig sowie der Schüler des Gymnasiums Bühlau dienen und ein weiterer Baustein ihrer Allgemeinbildung sein, da das Fach Astronomie seit 2007 aus dem Lehrplan gestrichen ist. Aber auch den Grundschulen Weißig und Schönfeld sowie anderen Einrichtungen wird die

Sternwarte zur Verfügung gestellt werden. Auch Hobbyastronomen und interessierten Bürgern wird die Sternwarte nicht verschlossen bleiben.
Das Jahr 2009 ist zum Internationalen Jahr der Astronomie erklärt worden. Deshalb hat sich der Verein das anspruchsvolle Ziel gesetzt, die Sternwarte im
IV. Quartal 2009 einweihen zu wollen. Zur Zeit ist die Sternwarte vollkommen entkernt. Sie muss bauseitig saniert werden, die Kuppel ist wieder gangbar zu machen und sämtliche Medien müssen verlegt werden.
Dafür benötigen wir aber unbedingt Verbündete, die uns besonders finanziell unterstützen. Neben der Interessengemeinschaft „Sternwarte Gönnsdorf", die Hobbyastronomen und interessierte Bürger vereint, wurde für Förderer und Spender ein „Freundeskreis Sternwarte Gönnsdorf" gegründet, der Spender und Förderer vereint, ohne weitere Verpflichtung.
Die Spenden werden selbstverständlich zweckgebunden für die Sternwarte eingesetzt und wären, sofern Sie es wollen, einmalig.

Der Verein zur Förderung der Jugend würde sich freuen, wenn Sie mit Ihrer Spende das Projekt „Sternwarte Gönnsdorf" unterstützen würden.

Juliane Vogt
Vorsitzende

Vorsitzender: Juliane Vogt
Geschäftskonto: 312 012 920 7BLZ: 850 503 00
Ostsächsische Sparkasse Dresden
Spendenkonto: 312 005 596 3 BLZ: 850 503 00
Ostsächsische Sparkasse Dresden

Amtsgericht Pirna VR-Nr. 305
Steuer Nummer: 11 202 143 01 831 63 0209

Verein
zur
Förderung
der
Jugend e.V.

Dresden, den 19.05.2009

Pillnitzer Str. 21c | 01328 Dresden / OT Weißig
(0351) 217 66 30
(0351) 217 66 31
@ vorstand@kjhpep.de

*Sternwarte Gönnsdorf*

Sehr geehrter Herr/ Frau ...

als Koordinatorin des Projektes „Sternwarte Gönnsdorf" des Vereins zur Förderung der Jugend e.V. und zugleich als Ortschaftsrätin darf ich Ihnen die Projektvorstellung der Vorsitzenden des Vereins, Frau Vogt, überreichen.

Die „Sternwarte Gönnsdorf" wurde ab 1970 von der TU Dresden aufgebaut. Sie ist sozusagen ein historisches Wahrzeichen im Schönfelder Hochland. Gemeinsam mit dem Ortsvorsteher, Herrn Behr, habe ich mich besonders für die Erhaltung dieses Wahrzeichens eingesetzt. Seit Anfang Januar 2009 gehört die Sternwarte nun dem Verein zur Förderung der Jugend e.V., der sich um eine vielfältige niveauvolle und interessante Freizeitgestaltung der Kinder und Jugendlichen im Schönfelder Hochland bemüht. Ein derartiges Freizeitangebot in den Abendstunden hat außerdem noch einen sozialen Aspekt.

Es ist ein besonderer Ansporn, im „Internationalen Jahr der Astronomie 2009" die Sternwarte bis zum Dezember 2009 wenigstens „startklar" zu machen.

Aber ohne Verbündete geht es leider nicht. Daher würden wir uns sehr freuen, wenn die Gewerbetreibenden des Schönfelder Hochlandes unsere Partner werden könnten und uns finanziell und/oder materiell unterstützen würden. Aus diesem Grund bitte ich Sie auch im Namen der Vorsitzenden des Vereins wohlwollend zu prüfen, ob Sie uns in geeigneter Form helfen können, unser Ziel zu erreichen.
Für Rückfragen stehe ich Ihnen unter Tel. 0351/2681272 gern zur Verfügung.

In der Hoffnung auf eine positive Entscheidung verbleibe ich
mit freundlichen Grüßen

Renate Franz

Vorsitzender: Juliane Vogt

| | |
|---|---|
| Geschäftskonto: | 312 012 920 7BLZ: 850 503 00<br>Ostsächsische Sparkasse Dresden |
| Spendenkonto: | 312 005 596 3 BLZ: 850 503 00<br>Ostsächsische Sparkasse Dresden |

Amtsgericht Pirna VR-Nr. 305
Steuer Nummer: 11 202 143 01 831 63 0209

---

## Observation Minutes

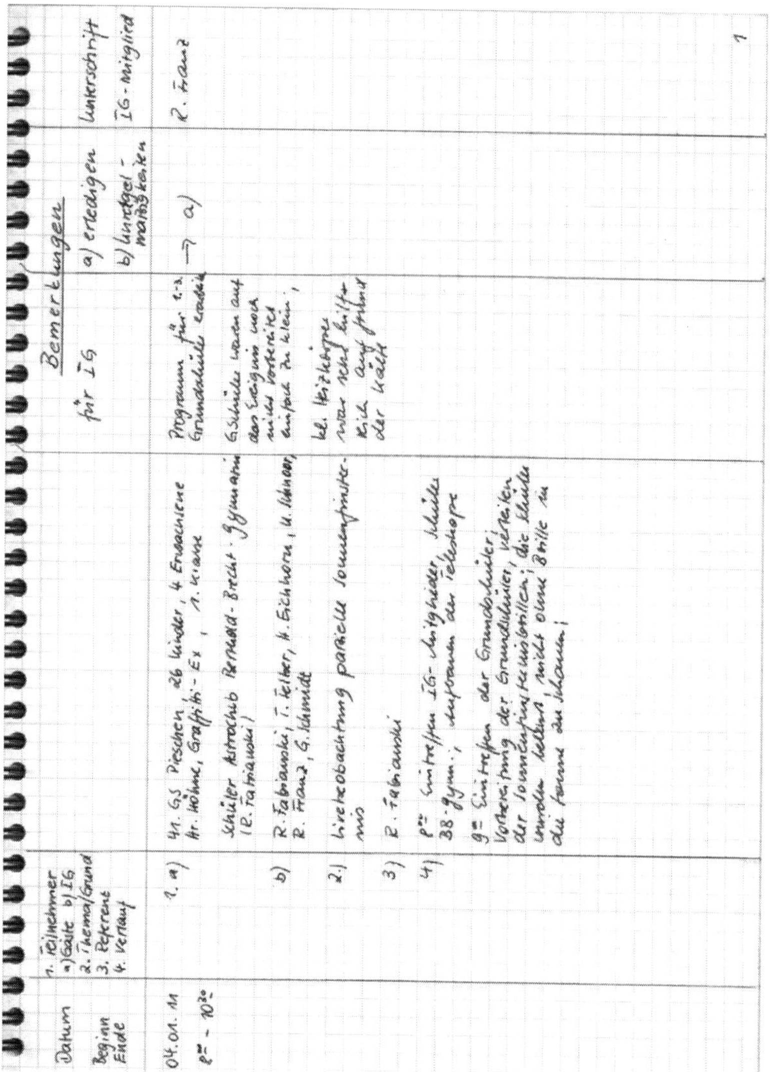

| Datum<br>Beginn<br>Ende | 1. Teilnehmer a) Gäste b) IG<br>2. Thema/Grund<br>3. Referent<br>4. Verlauf | | Bemerkungen<br>für IG | a) erledigen<br>b) Unregel-mäßigkeiten | Unterschrift<br>IG-Mitglied |
|---|---|---|---|---|---|
| 04.01.11<br>8⁰⁰ – 10³⁰ | 1. a) | 41. GS Pieschen, 26 Kinder, 4 Erwachsene<br>Hr. Höhne, Graffiti-Ex, 1. Klasse<br>Schüler Astroclub Bertolt-Brecht-Gymnasium (R. Fabianski) | Programm für 1.-3. Grundschüler erarbeiten | → a) | R. Franz |
| | b) | R. Fabianski, T. Felber, H. Eichhorn, U. Schnoor, R. Franz, G. Schmidt | Schüler waren auf das Ereignis noch nicht vorbereitet, einfach zu klein; | | |
| | 2.) | Livebeobachtung partielle Sonnenfinsternis | kl. Heizkörper war sehr hilfreich auf Grund der Kälte | | |
| | 3) | R. Fabianski | | | |
| | 4) | 8⁰⁰ Eintreffen IG-Mitglieder, Schüler 38. Gymn.; Aufbauen der Teleskope<br>9⁰⁰ Eintreffen der Grundschüler; Vorbereitung der Grundschüler, verteilen der Sonnenfinsternisbrillen; die Schüler wurden belehrt, nicht ohne Brille in die Sonne zu schauen; | | | |

1

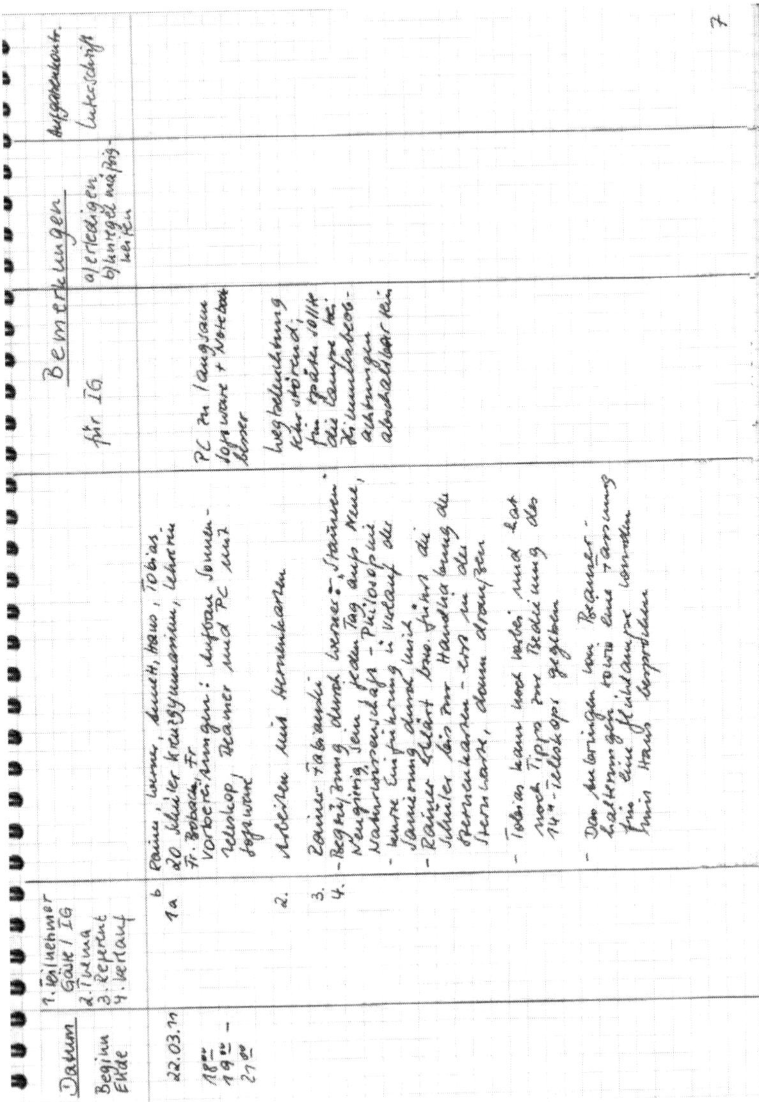

| Datum<br>Beginn<br>Ende | 1. Teilnehmer Gäste / IG<br>2. Thema<br>3. Referent<br>4. Verlauf | | Bemerkungen für IG | a) erledigen<br>b) Unregelmäßigkeiten | Aufgabenkontr.<br>Unterschrift |
|---|---|---|---|---|---|
| 22.03.11<br>18<br>19 –<br>21 | 1b<br>1a | Rainer, Werner, Annett, Hans, Tobias<br>20 Schüler Kreuzgymnasium, Lehrerin Fr. Bobach, Fr<br>Vorbereitungen: Aufbau Sonnen-Teleskop, Beamer und PC mit Software | PC zu langsam Software + Notebook besser | | |
| | 2. | Arbeiten mit Sternenkarten | Wegbeleuchtung sehr störend; für später sollte die Lampe bei Himmelsbeobachtungen abschaltbar sein | | |
| | 3.<br>4. | Rainer Fabianski<br>- Begrüßung durch Werner: „Staunen" Neugierig sein, jeden Tag aufs Neue, Naturwissenschaft – Philosophie<br>- kurze Einführung in Verlauf der Sanierung durch mich<br>- Rainer erklärt bzw. führt die Schüler bis zur Handhabung der Sternenkarten – erst in der Sternwarte, dann draußen<br>- Tobias kam noch vorbei und hat noch Tipps zur Bedienung des 14"-Teleskops gegeben<br>- Das Anbringen von Beamerhalterungen, sowie eine Fassung für eine Glühlampe wurden mit Hans besprochen | | | |

7

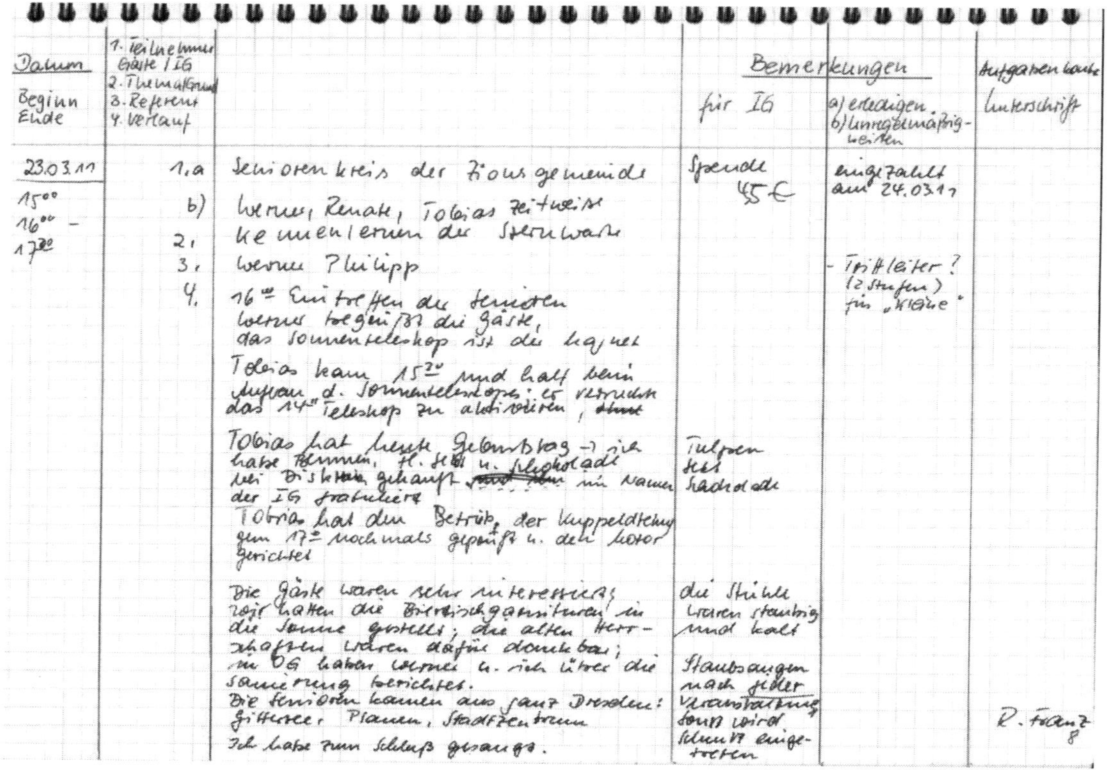

| Datum<br>Beginn<br>Ende | 1. Teilnehmer Gäste / IG<br>2. Thema/Grund<br>3. Referent<br>4. Verlauf | | Bemerkungen<br>für IG | a) erledigen<br>b) Unregelmäßigkeiten | Aufgaben kurz<br>Unterschrift |
|---|---|---|---|---|---|
| 23.03.17<br>15⁰⁰<br>16⁰⁰ –<br>17³⁰ | 1.a | Seniorenkreis der Zionsgemeinde | Spende 45 € | eingezahlt am 24.03.17 | |
| | b) | Werner, Renate, Tobias zeitweise | | | |
| | 2. | Kennenlernen der Sternwarte | | | |
| | 3. | Werner Philipp | | - Trittleiter? (2 Stufen) für „Kläre" | |
| | 4. | 16⁰⁰ Eintreffen der Senioren<br>Werner begrüßt die Gäste,<br>das Sonnenteleskop ist die Lagune | | | |
| | | Tobias kam 15³⁰ und half beim Aufbau d. Sonnenteleskops; er versuchte das 14" Teleskop zu aktivieren, ~~dann~~ | | | |
| | | Tobias hat heute Geburtstag → ich habe Blumen, H. Sekt u. Schokolade bei Diskothek gekauft ~~und~~ im Namen der IG gratuliert<br>Tobias hat den Betrieb der Kuppeldrehung um 17⁰⁰ nochmals geprüft u. den Motor gerichtet | Tulpen Sekt Schokolade | | |
| | | Die Gäste waren sehr interessiert; wir hatten die Biertischgarnituren in die Sonne gestellt; die alten Herrschaften waren dafür dankbar; im OG haben Werner u. ich über die Sammlung berichtet.<br>Die Senioren kamen aus ganz Dresden: Gittersee, Plauen, Stadtzentrum<br>Ich habe zum Schluß gesungen. | die Stühle waren staubig und kalt<br>Staubsaugen nach jeder Veranstaltung sonst wird Schmutz eingetreten | | R. Franz<br>8 |

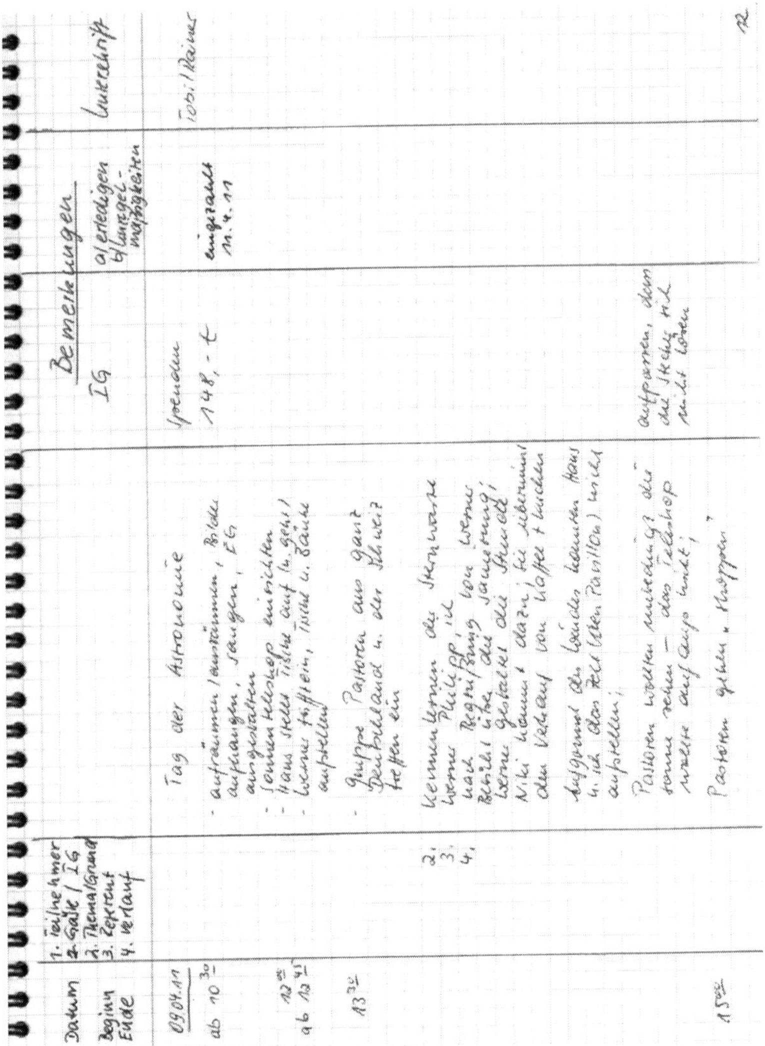

| Datum<br>Beginn<br>Ende | 1. Teilnehmer<br>2. Gäste / IG<br>2. Thema/Grund<br>3. Referent<br>4. Verlauf | | Bemerkungen<br>IG | a) erledigen<br>b) Unregelmäßigkeiten | Unterschrift |
|---|---|---|---|---|---|
| 09.04.11 | | Tag der Astronomie | Spenden | | Tobi / Rainer |
| ab 10$^{30}$ | | - aufräumen / ausräumen, Bilder aufhängen, saugen, EG ausgestalten<br>- Sonnenteleskop einrichten | 148,- € | eingezahlt 11.4.11 | |
| 12$^{00}$ | | - Hans stellt Tische auf (u. geht) | | | |
| ab 12$^{45}$ | | - Werner trifft ein, Tische u. Bänke aufstellen | | | |
| 13$^{30}$ | | - Gruppe Pastoren aus ganz Deutschland u. der Schweiz treffen ein | | | |
| | 2.<br>3.<br>4. | Kennenlernen die Sternwarte<br>Werner Philipp, ich<br>nach Begrüßung von Werner Bericht über die Sanierung; Werner gestaltet die Stunde<br>Niki kommt dazu; sie übernimmt den Verkauf von Kaffee + Kuchen | | | |
| | | Aufgrund des Windes konnten Hans u. ich das Zelt (den Pavillon) nicht aufstellen; | | | |
| | | Pastoren wollten unbedingt die Sonne sehen – das Teleskop wollte auf Anhieb nicht; | aufpassen, dass die Stecker sich nicht lösen | | |
| 15$^{00}$ | | Pastoren gehen „shoppen" | | | |

12

| Datum<br>Beginn<br>Ende | 1) Teilnehmer Gäste/ IG<br>2) Grund/ Thema<br>3) Referent<br>4) Verlauf | Bemerkungen für IG | a) unregelmäßig<br>b) erledigen | Unterschrift |
|---|---|---|---|---|
| 15.06.11<br>$19^{00}$<br>$24^{00}$ | 1) Interessierte „Mondgucker", Astrokurs BB-Gymn., Rainer, Christoph, Annett, Michaela, Niki, Hans, Werner, Nico, Tobias, Renate<br>2) totale Mondfinsternis<br>3) Rainer: „Hans guck in den Himmel"<br>Christoph: unser Mond 2x<br>4) - Sternwarte vorbereiten für Besucher<br>- ab $20^{00}$ für Gäste offen + Beobachtg.<br>- Teleskope wurden vor der Sternwarte postiert, um das Ereignis zu verfolgen. Hans + Tobias brachten eigene Teleskope mit = 8 Teleskope!<br>Nach und nach trafen die Besucher ein; u.a. auch vom Umweltamt (Herr von Strauwitz), so dass ich Gelegenheit hatte, unser „Bauvorhaben" vor Ort zu erläutern → es möge wirken!<br>• Christoph's Vortrag zum Mond kam sehr gut an;<br>- Alle Besucher + IG waren voller Hoffnung, dass sich wenigstens für einen kurzen Moment die Wolkendecke öffnet. Leider vergebens, so dass gegen $23^{30}$ die Besucher enttäuscht nach Hause fuhren. $23^{30}$ kamen noch Tobias Eltern vorbei → aber das half auch nicht mehr.<br>Rainer + Tobias halfen beim Aufräumen. | - die Vorbereitung für eine „offene" Sternwarte stehen meistens genügend IG-Mitglieder bereit<br>- für die Nachbereitung müssen/sollten Absprachen vor der Veranstaltung getroffen werden, wer bis zum Schluss bleibt, so zu sagen als „Aufräumkom."<br><br>Spende<br>25,- € | → TOP für IG-Treffen am 27.6.11<br><br>eingezahlt am 20.06.11 | R. Franz<br>22 |

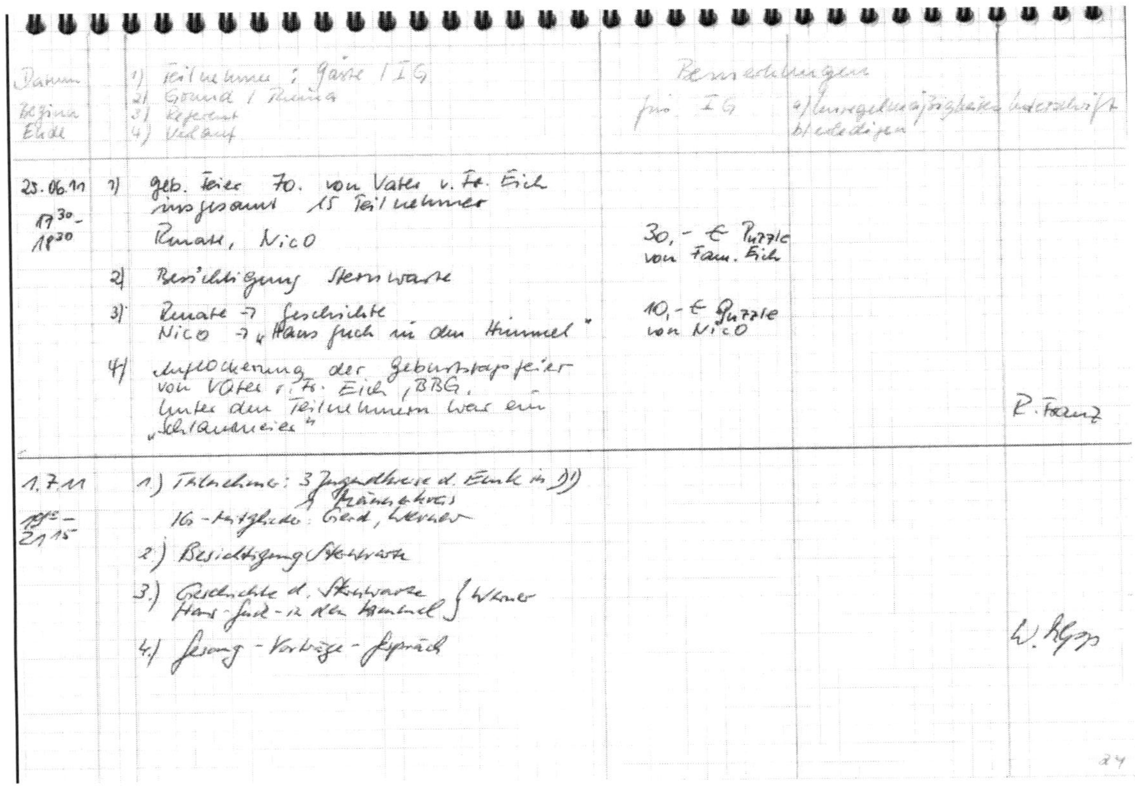

| Datum<br>Beginn<br>Ende | 1) Teilnehmer: Gäste / IG<br>2) Grund / Thema<br>3) Referent<br>4) Verlauf | Bemerkungen<br>pro IG | a) Unregelmäßigkeiten<br>b) erledigen | Unterschrift |
|---|---|---|---|---|
| 23.06.11<br>17³⁰–<br>18³⁰ | 1) geb. Feier 70. von Vater v. Fr. Eich<br>insgesamt 15 Teilnehmer<br>Renate, Nico<br>2) Besichtigung Sternwarte<br>3) Renate → Geschichte<br>Nico → „Hans guck in den Himmel"<br>4) Auflockerung der Geburtstagsfeier von Vater v. Fr. Eich, BBG.<br>Unter den Teilnehmern war ein „Schlaumeier" | 30,– € Puzzle von Fam. Eich<br><br>10,– € Puzzle von Nico | | R. Franz |
| 1.7.11<br>19⁰⁰–<br>21¹⁵ | 1.) Teilnehmer: 3 Jugendliche d. Einr. in DD<br>1 Männerkreis<br>IG-Mitglieder: Gerd, Werner<br>2.) Besichtigung Sternwarte<br>3.) Geschichte d. Sternwarte<br>Hans-guck-in-den-Himmel } Werner<br>4.) Gesang – Vorträge – Gespräch | | | W. Klopp |

24

| Datum<br>Beginn<br>Ende | | 1) Teilnehmer, Gäste / IG<br>2) Grund / Thema<br>3) Referent<br>4) Verlauf | Bemerkungen für IG | a) Unregelmäßigkeiten<br>b) erledigen | Unterschrift |
|---|---|---|---|---|---|
| 05.07.11 | | Kindergartengruppe „Leuchtturm", ca 20 Kinder –<br>Sonne, Mond u. Sterne – so groß ist das All<br>W. Philipp, A. [illegible]<br>Sagen, Vortrag „Hans guck...", Vorführung [illegible] u. Kuppel | | | |
| 06.7.11 | | Anett + Michaele – Probedurchlauf 1) „Sonnenteleskop" 2) 14" | Teleskop wieder abgedeckt | | [illegible] |
| 07.7.11 | | Renate → „Papiergegenstände" verstaut wegen des angesagten Gewitters | | a) Deckenlicht brennt | Renate |
| 08.07.11 | 1)<br>2) | Renate, Jürgen + Gäste<br>Besichtigung | 10 € Spende | | Renate |
| 12.07.11 | 1)<br>2) | Tobias, Jürgen, Renate<br>Ursachenforschung für „unrunde" Motorbewegungen<br>Platten mit Sprühöl „benetzt" | | b) 2 stärkere Federn besorgen<br>→ erst probieren | Renate |
| 14.7.11 | 1)<br>2) | Tobias, Jürgen, Renate<br>Federn ausprobieren (von Jürgen) | | Federn besorgen | Renate 25 |

## Lecture Program

Die Interessengemeinschaft Sternwarte Dresden-Gönnsdorf
stellt sich vor

am 20.11.2009, 19.00 Uhr
im Gasthaus zum Hochland, Dresden-Gönnsdorf

### Ablauf

Begrüßung
Essen bestellen (wer möchte)

**Vorstellung der 13 Mitglieder**

anschließend
Beiträge zu den Themen:

**Nutzung der Sternwarte für die außerschulische Weiterbildung**
Annett Miedtank, Christa Mikut

**Der Mond**
Prof. Christoph Metzner

**Das Apollo-Programm**
Eberhard Tremel

**Astronomische Zusammenhänge in der Bibel**
Pastor Werner Philipp

**Ein Hobbyastronom stellt seine Sternwarte vor**
Tobias Felber

**am Klavier Tim Dorn**

Die Mitglieder der IG Sternwarte Dresden-Gönnsdorf
wünschen
einen interessanten und angenehmen Abend.

## Survey Form

**Fragen zum Diskurs zwischen Religion und Naturwissenschaft***

Name (kann auch anonym bleiben):.......................................

Alter:..................................

Beruf/Fach:...........................

Weltanschauung/ Religion/ Konfession:...................................

1.) Sind Sie für eine strikte Trennung von Religion und Naturwissenschaft?

**Ja/ Nein** Begründen Sie kurz Ihre Meinung?

2.) Würden Sie sagen, dass die Naturwissenschaften die Wirklichkeit der Welt und des Universums umfassend zu beschreiben vermögen?

**Ja/ Nein** Wenn nicht, welche Instanzen kämen noch in Frage?

3.) Kann man Ihrer Meinung nach aus naturwissenschaftlichen Forschungsergebnissen ableiten, dass es keinen Gott gibt?

**Ja/ Nein**

4.) Haben sich Ihnen bei der Beschäftigung mit Astronomie und der Beobachtung von Himmelskörpern schon einmal philosophische, theologische oder ethische Fragen gestellt? Wenn ja, welche?

**Ja/ Nein**

5.) Wer ist nach Ihrer Ansicht für die Beantwortung von Sinn-, Werte- und ethischen Fragen zuständig?

6.) Ist Ihnen die Weltanschauung eines Wissenschaftlers wichtig?

**Ja/ Nein** Wenn er oder sie sich zu weltanschaulichen und ethischen Fragen äußert, inwieweit messen Sie diesen Aussagen besondere Glaubwürdigkeit zu?

7.) Sollte die Theologie naturwissenschaftliche Erkenntnisse berücksichtigen und in ihre Aussagen einbeziehen?

**Ja/ Nein** Inwieweit müssen sich Glaubensaussagen genauso an der Erfahrung messen lassen wie naturwissenschaftliche Beobachtungen?

8.) Sind Naturgesetze aus Ihrer Sicht immer und überall gültig?

**Ja/ Nein** Was halten Sie von Wundern und was verstehen Sie darunter?

9.) Wie beurteilen Sie das Verhältnis von Religion und Naturwissenschaft in Geschichte und Gegenwart? Können Sie für Ihre Position ein exemplarisches Beispiel nennen?

10.) Wie kann der Dialog zwischen Naturwissenschaft und Religion in Gang gesetzt bzw. intensiviert werden? Was wünschen Sie sich von den beiden Dialogpartnern?

***Vielen Dank für Ihre Mitwirkung!***

**Die Umfrage ist Bestandteil einer Doctor-of-Ministry-Dissertation von Werner Philipp, deren Ergebnisse in Auszügen veröffentlicht wird. Persönliche Angaben werden nicht oder nur anonymisiert abgedruckt.*

## BIBLIOGRAPHY

### Quoted Literature:

Bauer, Walter. *Wörterbuch zum Neuen Testament*. Berlin: Walter De Gruyter, 1971.

Bartel, Jörg. *Denkender Glaube: Unwissenschaftliche Anmerkungen zum Verhältnis von Glaube und Naturwissenschaft*, in: *Theologie für die Praxis, 36.Jg. 2010 Heft 3/2*. Göttingen: Edition Ruprecht, 2010.

Becker, Patrick. *Kein Platz für Gott? Theologie im Zeitalter der Naturwissenschaften*. Regensburg: Verlag Heinrich Pustet, 2009.

Benz, Arnold. *Die Zukunft des Universums: Zufall, Chaos, Gott?* Düsseldorf: Patmos Verlag, 1997.

Crutchfield, Leslie R., McLeod Grant, Heather. *Forces for Good: The Six Practices of High-Impact Nonprofits.* San Franzisco, CA: Jossey-Bass, 2008.

Bieritz, Karl-Heinrich. *Das Kirchenjahr: Feste, Gedenk- und Feiertage in Geschichte und Gegenwart*. Berlin: Union Verlag, 1988.

Bonhoeffer, Dietrich. *Letters and Papers from Prison*, ed. Eberhard Bethge, new
greatly enlarged ed. New York: Touchstone, 1997.

Brazos, R.R. Reno. *Theological Commentary on the Bible: Genesis*. Grand Rapids, MI: Brazos Press, 2010.

Conrad, J. et al.. *Das Alte Testament mit Erklärungen 1*. Berlin: Evangelische Haupt-Bibelgesellschaft, 1982.

Custer, Steward. *The Stars Speak: Astronomy in the Bible*. 2nd ed. Greenville/SC: Bob Jones University Press, 2002.

DeYoung, Donald B. *Astronomy and the Bible*. Wimona Lake, IN: BMH Books, 2010.

Diekmann, Friedrich. *Die unbegriffene Elbhangkugel: Manfred von Ardenne in Sinop und in Dresden*, in: *Dresden – Stadt der Wissenschaften, Dresdner Hefte Nr.86*. Dresden: Grafischer Betrieb und Verlagsgesellschaft mbH, 2006.

Dürr, Meyer-Abich, Mutschler, Pannenberg, Wuketits. *Gott, der Mensch und die Wissenschaft*. Augsburg: Pattloch Verlag, 1997.

Eichhorn, Hans-Jürgen. *Sternwarte- Dresden-Gönnsdorf – Chronik*. self-published, undated.

Evangelisch-methodistische Kirche. *OJK, Verhandlungen der 44.Tagung gehalten in Crottendorf 25.Mai-29.Mai 2011: Statistik des Jahres 2010.*

Evangelisch-methodistische Kirche in Deutschland, Österreich und Schweiz/ Frankreich. *Gesangbuch der Evangelisch-methodistischen Kirche*. Stuttgart: Medienwerk der Evangelsich-methodistischen Kirche GmbH, 2002.

Fischer, Ernst-Peter. *Von ästhetischen Momenten und poetischen Potentialen der Wissenschaft*, in: *Dresden – Stadt der Wissenschaften, Dresdner Hefte Nr.86*. Dresden: Grafischer Betrieb und Verlagsgesellschaft mbH, 2006.

Fohrer, Georg. *Kommentar zum Alten Testament: Das Buch Hiob*. 2nd ed. Berlin: Evangelische Verlagsanstalt GmbH, 1988.

Friedrich, Lutz. *Autobiographie und Religion der Spätmoderne: Biographische Suchbewegungen im Zeitalter transzendentaler Obdachlosigkeit*. Stuttgart: Kohlhammer, 1999.

Fuchs, Gotthard Fuchs. *Messe über die Welt,* in: *Das Herz des Universums- Einstein und die Frage nach Gott*, Extra-Heft: Christ in der Gegenwart. Freiburg: Herder, 2005.

German Bundestag. *Lebenslagen in Deutschland – Dritter Armuts- und Reichtumsbericht*. Deutscher Bundestag Drucksache 16/9915, 30 June 2008.

Gesenius, Wilhelm. *Hebräisches und aramäisches Handwörterbuch über das Alte Testament*. Berlin: Springer-Verlag, 1962.

Gingerich, Owen. *God's Universe.* Cambridge, MA: Havard University Press, 2006.

Gitt, Werner. *Signale aus dem All: Wozu gibt es Sterne*. 4th ed. Bielefeld: CLV Verlag, 2004.

Groody, Daniel E. *Globalization, Spirituality, and Justice*. New York: Maryknoll, 2010.

Guder, Darell L. *Missional Church*. Grand Rapids, MI: William B. Erdmann Publishing Company, 1998.

Hauerwas, Stanley. *Brazos Theological Commentary on The Bible: Matthew*. 2nd ed. Grand Rapids, MI: Brazos Press, 2009.

Jenni, Ernst/ Westerman, Claus. *Theologisches Handwörterbuch zum Alten Testament I+II*. München: Chr. Kaiser Verlag, 1984.

Hänseroth, Thomas. *"Nützliche Wissenschaften" in Dresden im 18. und frühen 19.Jahrhundert*, in: *Dresden – Stadt der Wissenschaften, Dresdner Hefte Nr.86*. Dresden: Grafischer Betrieb und Verlagsgesellschaft mbH, 2006.

Herrmann, Dieter B. *Entdecker des Himmels*. 4thed. Leipzig: Urania-Verlag, 1990.

Küng, Hans. *Der Anfang aller Dinge: Naturwissenschaft und Religion*. München: Piper Verlag, 2008.

Maunder, E. Walter E. *The Astronomy of the Bible*. ed. 2009 La Vergne, TN: Wildside Press, 1908.

Landeshauptstadt Dresden. *Focus on Dresden: The capital of Saxony in figures – 2011*. 19th [updated] ed. Dresden: designXpress dresden, 2011

Lebkücher, Anja. *Theologie der Natur: Wolfhart Pannenbergs Beitrag zum Dialog zwischen Theologie und Naturwissenschaft.* Neukirchen-Vluyn: Neukirchener Verlagsgesellschaft, 2011.

Mauersberger, Klaus. *Große Köpfe Dresdner Ingenieurwissenschaften.* in: *Dresden – Stadt der Wissenschaften, Dresdner Hefte Nr.86.* Dresden: Grafischer Betrieb und Verlagsgesellschaft mbH, 2006

Moltmann, Jürgen. *God in Creation: A New Theology of Creation and the Spirit of God.* Minneapolis, MN: Fortress Press, 1993.

Mühlen, Heribert. *Neu mit Gott.* Freiburg: Herder-Verlag, 2000.

Mutschler, Hans Dieter. *Physik und Christentum – Auferstehung von der Festplatte. Religiöse Weihe für den Fortschritt: Zu Frank Tiplers Buch "Die Physik der Unsterblichkeit"* in: Publik-Forum 12/1994. Oberursel: Public-Forum Verlagsgesellschaft mbH, 1994.

Henri.J.M. Nouwen. *Leben hier und jetzt.* Freiburg: Herder-Verlag, 2000.

Oschwald, Hanspeter. *Glaube in Deutschland.* München: Focus/Meyers Lexikonverlag, 1999.

Pannenberg Wolfhart. *Toward a Theology of Nature: Essays on Science and Faith.* Louisville, KT: Westminster/John Knox Press, 1993.

_____. *Systematic Theology Vol.2.* Edinburgh: T&T Clark Ltd., 1994.

Ivan Petrella. *Beyond Liberation Theology: A Polemic.* London: SCM Press, 2008.

Polkinghorne, John. *Science and Theology: An Introduction*. Minneapolis, MN: Fortress Press, 1998.

____. *Theology in the Context of Science*. London: SPCK, 2008.

von Rad, Gerhard. *Das erste Buch Mose, ATD 2*. Göttingen: Vandenhoek & Ruprecht, 1949.

Karl Rahner. *Schriften zur Theologie Bd. VII*. Einsiedeln: Benzinger, 1966

Reschika, Richard. *Praxis christlicher Mystik: Einübung von den Wüstenvätern bis zur Gegenwart*. Freiburg: Herder, 2007.

Kotter, John P. *Leading Change*. Bosten, MA: Havard Business School Press, 1996.

Tiefensee, Eberhard, Sporer, Tabea. *Konfessionslosigkeit ein Ostdeutsches Phänomen?* in: Christen in der Offensive e.V. (Hrsg.), *Brennpunkt Seelsorge, Heft 1/2003*. Reichelsheim, 2003

Tipler, Frank J. *The Physics of Immortality*. New York: Doublesday, 1994.

Tipler, Frank J. *Die Physik der Unsterblichkeit: Moderne Kosmologie, Gott und Auferstehung der Toten*. München: R.Piper GmbH & Co. KG, 1994.

Tomka, Miklós, Zulehner, Paul. *Religion in den Reformländern Ost- (Mittel) Europas*. Wien/Ostfildern: Schwabenverlag, 1999.

Vlk, Miloslav Kardinal. *Also avanti! - Christentum und Kirche im Gegenwind der Zeit*. Leipzig: Benno-Verlag, 1999.

Wanke, Joachim, Hrsg. EMW, ACK, Missio. *Aufbruch zu einer missionarischen Ökumene: Ein Verständigungsprozess über die gemeinsame Aufgabe der Mission und Evangelisation in Deutschland*. Hamburg: Brcklumer Druckerei Manfred Siegel KG. 1999.

Weems, Lovett H. *Take the next step: Leading lasting change in the Church*. Nashville, TN: Abingdon Press, 2003.

Weigert, A./ Zimmermann, H. *Brockhaus ABC Astronomie*. 7th ed. Leipzig: F.A.Brockhaus Verlag, 1976.

Weinberg, Steven. *The Fist Three Minutes*. New York: Pantheon, 1977.

von Weizsäcker, Carl Friedrich. *Die Einheit der Natur*. 2nd ed. München: Carl Hanser Verlag, 1981

Westermann, Claus. *Schöpfung*. Stuttgart: Kreuz-Verlag, 1983.

Wilkinson, David. *Christian Eschatology and the Physical Universe*. London: T&T Clark Int'l, 2010.

**Quoted Websites:**

http://www.asa3.org/ASA/PSCF/1995/PSCF12-95Haas.html
Haas, J.W. Jr. *John Wesley's Vision of Science in the Service of Christ*. last access: 01 November 2011

http://www.astronomy2009.org
last access: 17 December 2011

http://www.astronomy2009.org/general/
last access: 17 December 2011

http://www.astronomy2009.org/news/updates/682/
last access: 29 January 2012

http://www.bibelwissenschaft.de/nc/wibilex/das-bibellexikon/details/quelle/WIBI/referenz/27985/cache/f1e54767c88d7b9247677cfa360180dc/
Gabriele Theuer, *Das wissenschaftliche Bibellexikon im Internet: Der Mond*.
last access: 12 October 2011

http://www.dresden.de/de/03/kirchen.php
last access: 10 December 2011

http://www.dresden.de/media/pdf/statistik/Dresdner_Zahlen_aktuell_17_2010_07.pdf
last access: 10 December 2011

http://www.dresden.de/media/pdf/statistik/11__ussere_Neustadt.pdf
last access: 10 December 2011

http://www.gbz-emmaus.de/geschichte.php
last access: 4 December 2011

http://www.gbz-emmaus.de/predigt-mp3.php
last access: 10 January 2012

http://www.jewishencyclopedia.com/view.jsp?artid=2052&letter=A#6263
last access: 27 September 2011

http://www.kirchenaustritt.de/statistik/#Religionszugehoerigkeit_in_Deutschland
last access: 10 December 2011

http://www.kjhpep.de/index.php?start
last access: 16 December 2011

http://www.stadtjugendring-dresden.de/index.php?id=14,36,0,0,1,0
last access: 16 December 2011

http://www.sternwarte-goennsdorf.de
last access: 29 January 2012

http://www.sternwarte-goennsdorf.de/puzzle.php
last access: 22 December 2011

http://www.sternwarte-goennsdorf.de/sponsoren.php
last access: 29 January 2011

http://www.sternwarte-goennsdorf.de/vorgeschichte.php
last access: 13 December 2011

http://www.wesnex.org/H_AboutUs_History_WesleyScience.html
last access: 1 November 2011

19020350R00097

Made in the USA
Middletown, DE
04 April 2015